ROCK
Knebworth
FESTIVALS

CHRYSSIE LYTTON COBBOLD

Omnibus Press
LONDON·NEW YORK·SYDNEY·COLOGNE

Pages from the
Knebworth House
visitors' book.

This book is a personal memento of the festivals we have held at Knebworth over the past twelve years. Modern music is an international language that has done more for world peace than all the diplomats and politicians put together. A million people have attended the music festivals at Knebworth. My recollections in the pages that follow are dedicated to the fans who have sat in the sun or stood in the rain for the pleasure of great music played in one of the most beautiful natural concert arenas anywhere in the world.

We will always be grateful to Freddie and Wendy Bannister for persuading us to play host to rock festivals at Knebworth. From Adelaide to Santa Barbara, Stockholm to Nairobi, wherever I travel I discover Knebworth fans. In France this summer, sitting with a girlfriend in a deserted moonlit square at midnight, our peace was disturbed by a gang of rowdies swaying through the street shouting, 'Anyone got any grass in this Godforsaken town?' Our hearts sank. Spying us, we were surrounded and the usual harassment began. 'Where do you come from?' asked one. 'Near Stevenage', I replied. 'Never heard of it,' he said. 'Well...Knebworth,' I ventured. 'KNEBWORTH', they chorused. 'Deep Purple. F...ing wet wasn't it?' The aggressive mood became tranquil and the concert was discussed. As we left there were friendly shouts of 'See you next year'.

Outdoor rock concerts have a mixed reputation. Many local authorities have tried to stamp them out. They cite the noise, the mess, and thousands of hippies tramping over farmers' fields. Yes, they are noisy and there is a mess to clear up afterwards. But trouble there is not. Compared to football crowds, rock fans are peaceful and well behaved. They come to hear the music; and I hope they will continue to do so.

My comments on the groups and individuals that I have encountered at the festivals over the years are purely personal. I offer no apologies should they give offence to anyone.

I am grateful to the following for the use of photographs: Simon Scott, the North Herts Gazette, Capital Radio, the Welwyn Times, Henry Denison Pender and Tim Leach. My thanks also to David Campbell and Andy Hudson for additional material.

Chryssie Lytton Cobbold
Knebworth House
November, 1985

INTRODUCTION

KNEBWORTH ROCK FESTIVALS

© Copyright 1986 Omnibus Press
(A Division of Book Sales Limited)
Text © Copyright Christina Lytton Cobbold 1986

Edited by Chris Charlesworth
Art Direction by Mike Bell
Co-ordinated by Lynda Hassett
Book Designed by Stylo Rouge
Picture research by Chryssie Lytton Cobbold & Valerie Boyd

ISBN: 0.7119.0774.9
Order No: OP 43587

Exclusive distributors:
Book Sales Limited,
78 Newman Street, London W1P 3LA, UK.

Music Sales Corporation,
24 East 22nd Street, New York,
NY 10010, USA.

Omnibus Press,
GPO Box 3304, Sydney,
NSW 2001, Australia.

To the Music Trade only:
Music Sales Limited,
78 Newman Street, London W1P 3LA, UK.

Picture credits:
Robert Ellis: Pages 6, 7, 8, 10, 11, 18, 22, 26, 39,
40, 42, 44, 45, 46, 48, 59, 60, 61, 62, 63, 65, 66.
Relay Photos: Pages 7, 10, 11, 23, 42, 61,
63, 64, 66, 72, 93, 96.
Barry Plummer: Pages 9, 10, 12/13, 18, 19, 21, 24, 25, 26,
27, 35, 36/37, 43, 45, 47, 48, 51, 52/53, 54, 55, 59, 62, 63.
David Redfern: Pages 46, 73, 74, 78, 80, 81.
Tom Sheehan: Pages 70, 71, 74.
Jon Blackmore: Pages 71, 72, 91, 94, 95.
Jak Kilby: Pages 76, 77, 78, 79, 80, 82.
Tom Hustler: Page 76.
Tony Motram: Pages 88, 89, 90, 92, 93.
North Herts Gazette: Page 90.
Ros Halfin: Page 96.

Typeset by floppy disc transfer by Serious Software.
Printed in Scotland by: Scotprint Limited, Musselburgh.

1974

ALLMAN BROTHERS

In early 1974 Freddie Bannister came into our office at Knebworth House. "I would like to hire the park for a rock festival in July," he said. "How much money would you want?" We said we were sorry, but the answer was no. We had been asked by promoters before about holding concerts in the park; we didn't think pop festivals were the right image for stately homes; we valued our local reputation too much and were also a trifle scared at the idea of having thousands of rock fans all over the park. We had always said no in the past.

But Freddie was very persuasive. Everything had a price, he said, and asked us to name ours. We suggested a five figure sum, never dreaming he would accept. But he did and before long we found ourselves famous the world over as a rock venue.

The concert that summer, known as the 'Bucolic Frolic', was planned for July 20. Headlines appeared in the local press as soon as the word was out. Figures of 25,000 fans coming to Knebworth were mentioned; then there was a rumour that Led Zeppelin were to head the bill, and it shot up to 100,000.

There were endless meetings with the promoter, the council, the police, the Red Cross, St Johns Ambulance, car parkers and more. Chief Superintendent Tom Oliver, head of North Herts Police Division, thought it would be a good exercise for his men; all leave was duly cancelled. Local shop keepers couldn't decide whether to lock and bar their premises against the invasion or stock up and possibly make a fortune. Worried parents rang us at the House. Would it be safe for their offspring to come to the Festival? I didn't know, I could only tell them that my own children would be there. Mr Rourke, owner of the deer in the park, wanted assurances that no one would interfere with his stock. We told him the crowds were coming to listen to the music, not to barbecue his deer (at least we hoped not).

Above: Van Morrison leads the Caledonia Soul Orchestra.

Above: John McLaughlin seeks spiritual bliss with his Mahavishnu Orchestra.
Below: Doobie Brother Tiran Porter

Although it was a one day concert starting at 10.30 a.m. and ending at 11 p.m. some fans were expected to arrive the day before and camp overnight, and possibly Saturday night as well. It was as if we needed to prepare for a town the size of Stevenage moving into the park for 48 hours and it required endless organisation. Two miles of corrugated fencing was needed to surround the arena, a stage had to be built, the sound system set up. Capable of 700 decibels, it threatened to be the loudest ever heard in England; 25,000 watts of sound – equal to the noise of seven low flying aircraft, or 25 full sized discotheques, seven times the accepted pain threshold!

Fifty ten-seater circular tin loos with awnings over them and canvas partitions had to be erected. Water taps, lighting, food, market stalls, Red Cross, St Johns Ambulance, fire engines and information centres all had to be organised and sited.

For a month before the concert the park was full of heavy machinery digging latrine pits and laying pipes, putting up marquees and mobile offices. The site crew camped in the park in tents and caravans, their washing, dogs and children very much in evidence. The meetings became more intense. Led Zeppelin dropped out, apparently because of recording and film commitments; Freddie Bannister was furious and threatened to sue them.

By June the line-up was finalised: The Allman Brothers Band, Van Morrison (featuring The New Caledonia Soul Express), The Doobie Brothers, John McLaughlin's latest Mahavishnu Orchestra, which included French violinist Jean Luc Ponty, Tim Buckley and The Alex Harvey Band. Tickets went on sale at £2.75 in advance and £3.00 on the day.

ALLMAN BROTHERS

1974

People started arriving a few days before the concert. The campsite wasn't ready and didn't open until Friday afternoon, and by that time there was already a substantial crowd. A steady stream of colourful people with knapsacks on their backs approached the park from all directions. Concerned that they might pitch their tents in some angry local resident's garden, I drove around collecting them up in my car and dropping them at the campsite. Eventually 25,000 people hitching to Knebworth was too much for my Renault, so I left them to walk.

The campsite on Friday night was a wonderful sight, a mass of coloured tents and small fires. Loads of firewood was provided in an attempt to prevent any pillage of the park trees. People played guitars and threw parties. There were two huge marquees for those without tents. It was a fine night, and the weather forecast was good.

The arena gates opened at 5 a.m. and by 7 a.m. the site was already fairly full. We made a family encampment with sleeping bags, rugs, and a long pole with a flag on top which would enable us to find our way back to it. Richard, my six year old, began playing 'snap' with a rock fan sitting on the grass next to us. He got into a heated argument. The man asked Richard where he lived and when he said "There", pointing to Knebworth House behind, the man said "Oh yeah, and I live in Buckingham Palace". "But I really do," protested Richard. "Tell me another," said the man. I don't think he ever believed him.

OFFICIAL VEHICLE PASS
FREDERICK BANNISTER'S BUCOLIC FROLIC JULY 20TH 1974

By midday the sun blazed down on 60,000 denim clad fans from all over the world, on the grass, sharing their drink and dope around. Babies ran naked around the site and dogs frolicked in the grass

Clockwise from top left: Alex Harvey swinging from the rafters; Chris Glen, Alex Harvey & Zal Cleminson; Zal Cleminson; Tim Buckley.

enjoying it all as much as anyone. The queues for the loos and hot dogs had started, as had the music. The atmosphere was pungent with the smell of bodies, beer, fish and chips, and exotic smoke.

Tim Buckley, the American songwriter, and his four piece band opened the first Knebworth Festival fifty minutes late due to technical problems. People were still arriving, finding friends and generally settling themselves down, so he didn't get everyone's attention. But his full-blooded and sensuous voice made an ideal start to the concert. As well as a singer, he was a poet and an arranger. He started off in his early teens singing in country bands, then moved to folk and jazz and rock and roll. Buckley was a serious musician and it showed in his performance.

After a short pause The Sensational Alex Harvey Band followed in grand eloquent contrast. Harvey, dressed in a black frock coat, jeans and jock strap, flexed a vicious cane, and his lead guitarist, Zal Cleminson, to his left, leapt about like a demon jester with his face made up in white pan stick and his tongue lolling lasciviously. They played the fool but they got away with it as their music was loud and dynamic. The audience started to join in, their sense of pace and timing with songs like 'Sergeant Fury' was perfect, and the fans loved it.

Between the acts, throughout the day, compères Pete Drummond and John Peel read out the usual garbled pleas for mislaid persons…would Dave please come to the information tent where his insulin is waiting for him? Lost children…Saffron four years old,

ALLMAN BROTHERS

1974

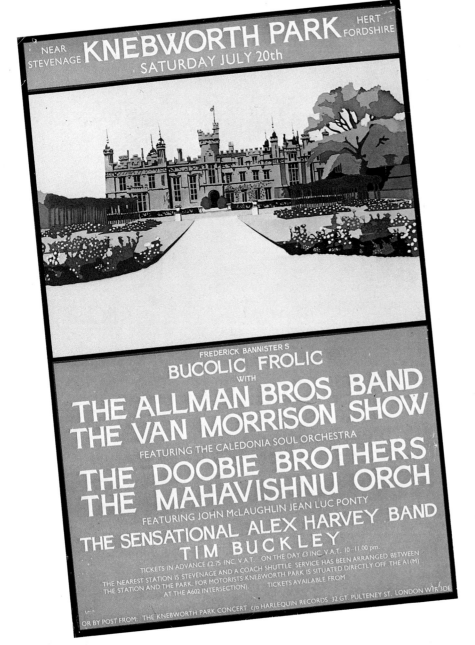

NEAR STEVENAGE **KNEBWORTH PARK** HERTFORDSHIRE

SATURDAY JULY 20th

FREDERICK BANNISTER'S

BUCOLIC FROLIC

WITH

THE ALLMAN BROS BAND
THE VAN MORRISON SHOW

FEATURING THE CALEDONIA SOUL ORCHESTRA

THE DOOBIE BROTHERS
THE MAHAVISHNU ORCH

FEATURING JOHN McLAUGHLIN JEAN LUC PONTY

THE SENSATIONAL ALEX HARVEY BAND
TIM BUCKLEY

TICKETS IN ADVANCE £2.75 INC. V.A.T. ON THE DAY £3 INC. V.A.T. 10 - 11.00 pm. THE NEAREST STATION IS STEVENAGE AND A COACH SHUTTLE SERVICE HAS BEEN ARRANGED BETWEEN THE STATION AND THE PARK. FOR MOTORISTS KNEBWORTH PARK IS SITUATED DIRECTLY OFF THE A1 (M) AT THE A602 INTERSECTION). TICKETS AVAILABLE FROM

OR BY POST FROM: THE KNEBWORTH PARK CONCERT c/o HARLEQUIN RECORDS 32 GT. PULTENEY ST. LONDON W1R 3DE

wearing a white dress… No alcohol was sold on site so people arrived with Tesco wire trolleys laden with wine, beer and cider, which they pushed two miles from Stevenage.

John McLaughlin's Mahavishnu Orchestra, resembling a walking Daz advertisement, came on stage next. Everything seemed to be played in a piercing tone and frequently reached the level of a shriek. McLaughlin called for a few seconds of reverent silence while they soaked up the atmosphere, but as everyone had come to hear music this didn't go down very well. But they had a huge following of fans and received a standing ovation. One man took off his sarong and danced naked in the crowd, doing his own thing and not caring who was staring. But it was all too technical for my tastes.

By now the queues for food were 150 yards long and, in spite of the 'Gully Cleanser' lorry emptying the loos at regular intervals, some were overflowing and loo paper had long since disappeared. 20,000 hot dogs, 15,000 fish and chips, 12,000 squashes and 6,000 hamburgers were consumed during the day. By 9 p.m. the caterers had run out of food. But the sun was shining and everyone seemed happy.

Left, top to bottom: John McLaughlin;
Tiran Porter; Van Morrison;
Alex Harvey.
Right: Tim Buckley; Alex Harvey;
Van Morrison; Tiran Porter.
Below: Jeff Baxter (Doobie Brothers);
Dickie Betts (Allman Brothers).

ALLMAN BROTHERS

1974

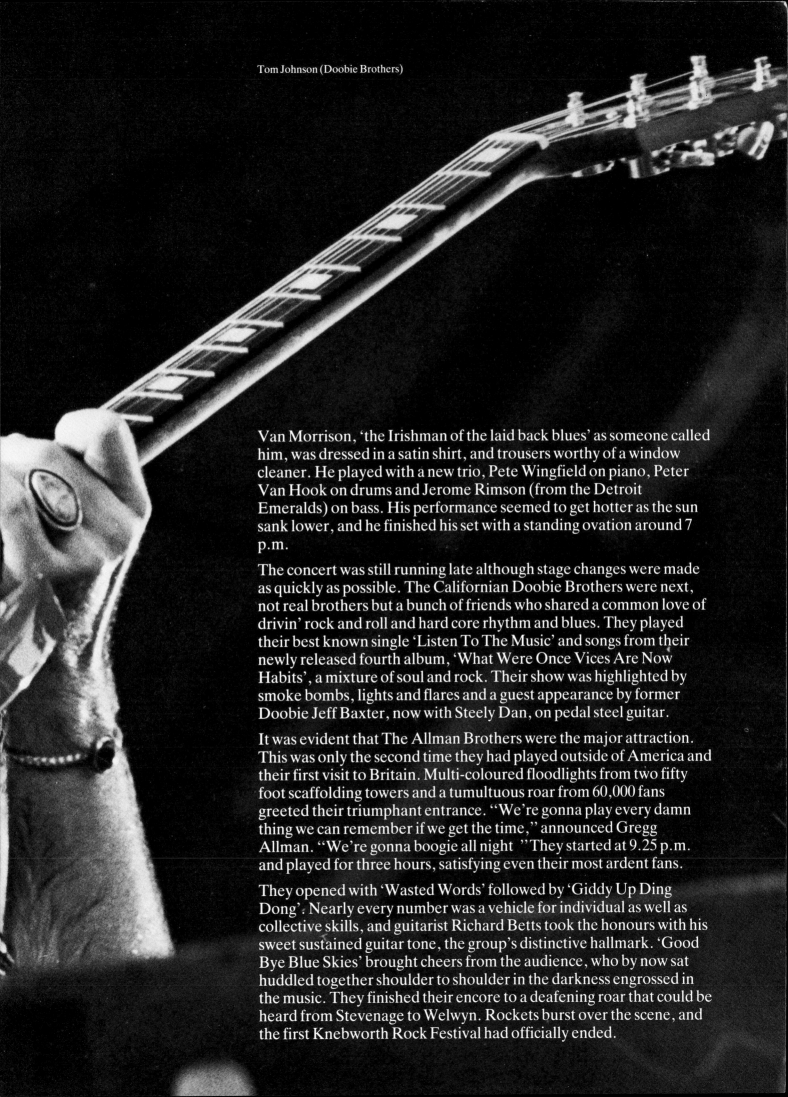

Tom Johnson (Doobie Brothers)

Van Morrison, 'the Irishman of the laid back blues' as someone called him, was dressed in a satin shirt, and trousers worthy of a window cleaner. He played with a new trio, Pete Wingfield on piano, Peter Van Hook on drums and Jerome Rimson (from the Detroit Emeralds) on bass. His performance seemed to get hotter as the sun sank lower, and he finished his set with a standing ovation around 7 p.m.

The concert was still running late although stage changes were made as quickly as possible. The Californian Doobie Brothers were next, not real brothers but a bunch of friends who shared a common love of drivin' rock and roll and hard core rhythm and blues. They played their best known single 'Listen To The Music' and songs from their newly released fourth album, 'What Were Once Vices Are Now Habits', a mixture of soul and rock. Their show was highlighted by smoke bombs, lights and flares and a guest appearance by former Doobie Jeff Baxter, now with Steely Dan, on pedal steel guitar.

It was evident that The Allman Brothers were the major attraction. This was only the second time they had played outside of America and their first visit to Britain. Multi-coloured floodlights from two fifty foot scaffolding towers and a tumultuous roar from 60,000 fans greeted their triumphant entrance. "We're gonna play every damn thing we can remember if we get the time," announced Gregg Allman. "We're gonna boogie all night " They started at 9.25 p.m. and played for three hours, satisfying even their most ardent fans.

They opened with 'Wasted Words' followed by 'Giddy Up Ding Dong'. Nearly every number was a vehicle for individual as well as collective skills, and guitarist Richard Betts took the honours with his sweet sustained guitar tone, the group's distinctive hallmark. 'Good Bye Blue Skies' brought cheers from the audience, who by now sat huddled together shoulder to shoulder in the darkness engrossed in the music. They finished their encore to a deafening roar that could be heard from Stevenage to Welwyn. Rockets burst over the scene, and the first Knebworth Rock Festival had officially ended.

KNEBWORTH PARK
JULY 20th
SATURDAY

Frederick Bannister's
BUCOLIC FROLIC
WITH

THE ALLMAN BROTHERS BAND
THE VAN MORRISON SHOW
FEATURING THE CALEDONIA SOUL EXPRESS
THE DOOBIE BROTHERS
THE MAHAVISHNU ORCHESTRA
FEATURING JOHN McLAUGHLIN & JEAN LUC PONTY
THE SENSATIONAL ALEX HARVEY BAND
TIM BUCKLEY

TICKETS IN ADVANCE £2.75 ON THE DAY £3 INC. V.A.T. 10—11.00 pm. THE NEAREST STATION IS STEVENAGE AND A
COACH SHUTTLE SERVICE HAS BEEN ARRANGED BETWEEN THE STATION AND THE PARK.
FOR MOTORISTS KNEBWORTH PARK IS SITUATED DIRECTLY OFF THE A1(M) AT THE A602
TICKETS AVAILABLE FROM

BY POST FROM: THE KNEBWORTH PARK CONCERT c/o HARLEQUIN RECORDS 32 GT. PULTENEY ST. LONDON W1R 3DE

As 60,000 blanket clad punters filed out of the arena after midnight on Sunday morning, the general feeling seemed to be of bemused delight. Everyone had behaved well, the police and local authorities were pleased, the concert had been well organised. The litter was horrific. The Park and House were open to the public at 11 a.m. that morning. How were we going to clear it all up? My husband David and I got some black plastic bags and started on it; we soon realised the futility of our efforts and gave up.

It took hours to clear the park of vehicles. By 1 a.m., there was still a long queue for the special buses back to Stevenage Station. Dawn broke and the arena looked like a deserted battlefield. The bells for Sunday worship rang from the church in the park, a mother dressed in a bikini and blue wellies was bathing her small son in a horse trough, bodies began emerging from sleeping bags. Anyone willing to stay on and clear up the litter could earn 10p a bag. One girl, naked except for a sun hat and shoes, took a bag and started to pick up the rubbish. Two bored and tired security men guarding the Allman Brothers' Steinway piano on stage woke up, yawned and shouted for breakfast.

There were rave reviews about the concert in the papers. Even the hawkish New Musical Express was polite. "If Buxton was beastly and Olympia just plain limp, then even the gloomiest of us have to admit the Knebworth Festival was indeed pretty Knice. So they do work after all. We always knew they could".

The only complaint seemed to be that ratepayers would have to foot the bill for the police and litter clearing in Stevenage and Knebworth, a sum in the region of £10,000. The police didn't charge for their presence at the concert because, as Councillor W.A. Hill of Hitchin told the Herts County Council, "No charge was made upon the organisers for police as they hired civilian security staff for the area to which admission by payment was made…" Unfortunately this attitude didn't prevail in the years that followed.

Less than 30 arrests were made; 480 people were treated for minor ailments, sunburn, headaches and stings. Only 20 casualties went to hospital, the most serious case a fracture. There had been 300 St. Johns Ambulance and Red Cross personnel on duty, 6 doctors, 20 State Registered Nurses and 16 ambulances, five of them permanently manned.

One group of hippies decided Knebworth Park was an ideal place to live and ignored our requests to leave after the concert. The weather was fine and they wandered around their encampment with little or nothing on. We eventually helped them pack up their belongings, drove them to Stevenage station and dropped them off to catch a train. They were back in the park again by the time we got back! So we piled them back into a van, actually bought them tickets and saw them on to the train to London. This time they didn't return.

Before the war David's grandfather, Lord Lytton, put up the following notice in the park:

TO VISITORS

*All ye who enter Knebworth Park
One moment pause these words to mar
This property belongs to me
As visitors here welcome be
As you proceed please feel a duty
Not to disfigure Nature's beauty
With remnants of a picnic meal
Silver paper or orange peel.
If you are smokers be so kind
As not to leave a trail behind
Of cigarette cards, matches, rags
Empty packets or paper bags.
If you have such litter, leave it
In baskets furnished to receive it.
Give no one cause to think you hateful
And I the owner will be grateful,
And ever gladly make you free
Of places that are loved by me.*

LYTTON.

Someone added to this after a concert

*Don't leave your roaches in the grass
It's best to stash them in your boxes
Remember all you doped buffoons
The Lord won't take to coker's spoons
And if you feel the urge to mate
To procreate, to copulate
Just think, not all will have your luck
There'll be some bad vibes if you…
(get down and get with it.)*

ANON.

1975

PINK FLOYD

By April the second Knebworth Rock Festival was under way. Our music and dancing licence for the park was limited to 15,000, so this year we had to ask North Herts Council for an extension to the existing licence for the day.

There was strong opposition from some councillors and several conditions were imposed. The noise would be limited to a level acceptable to the Environmental Health Officer; extra lighting would be provided to facilitate the safe departure of fans; the concert could not begin before noon and would finish promptly by 11 p.m. with a fine if the music overran. A sum of £5,000 would be needed from the promoters to pay any extra costs that might occur.

The licence for 40,000 people was eventually granted for July 5. There was very little opposition from the local residents. They mostly agreed that fans were well behaved the year before and though the music was loud it was only for one day, and they could stand that. In fact, some sat in their gardens and enjoyed it. Shopkeepers and public houses in the area were delighted; the ones who stayed open the previous year had made a fortune. Everywhere I went people asked me if there was going to be a concert again this year. They all hoped there would be.

The bands would be limited to just five, so as to prevent last year's late night running. There were many rumours going around as to the line-up – Lynyrd Skynyrd, Paul McCartney and Wings, The Who. At last Tedoar Ltd (Freddie Bannister's newly formed company) announced the programme. Pink Floyd was to top the bill; they had just embarked upon a mammoth US tour, but were due to return to Britain in the summer. The rest of the line-up was The Steve Miller Band, Captain Beefheart and his Magic Band, Roy Harper, Linda Lewis, and as special guests, Graham Chapman (with friends) from Monty Python. The compère was disc jockey John Peel. Tickets were £2.75 in advance and £3.00 on the day.

Left: Pink Floyd's backdrop screen.
Above: Roy Harper at play.
Below: Roger Waters at work.

As an experiment, camping was allowed inside the park this year but space was limited and people were urged to come just for the day. The police decided to take over car parking and traffic control inside the park, as well as outside; a mistake, as we discovered to our cost. Showex constructed a huge covered stage 30 metres by 90 metres, designed to carry heavy loads of equipment. The roof, 13.4 metres above stage level, had a clear span of 15.2 metres. They provided an electric hoist for lifting heavy musical instruments and speaker cabinets on to the stage. We were used to the general upheaval in the park so this time we did not worry unduly.

The concert was a sell out. Despite warnings on national pop radio throughout the week before not to turn up in the hope of buying tickets on the day as there would be no gate sales, fans still turned up in their thousands. People poured in all night. By 10 a.m., all roads to Knebworth were blocked, the queue went all the way back to Hatfield, 10 miles south, and 6 miles north on the A1 motorway. Numerous breakdowns added to the confusion. My husband David was not happy, and blamed the police. Some of the problem was caused by camping in the park, pedestrians had to cross the flow of traffic to reach the festival site, and this occasionally halted the traffic flow completely.

PINK FLOYD

1975

Inside the arena hundreds of colourful flags bearing names, places, and mottoes, fluttered over a mass of bodies waiting for the concert to begin. From the year before I recognised 'Jesus', a kind of freelance philosopher and exhibitionist who turns up at all the festivals with his long blonde hair, royal blue singlet, beads and a large pink plastic flower. He'd worn a sarong and danced naked the previous year. The stalls were selling incense, badges, king-sized cigarette papers, frisbees and patchouli oil. Many people came prepared after last year's experience of food queues, and brought their own. The ones who hadn't complained of the prices: hot dogs at 15p each, cans of Coca Cola for 30p.

At noon Linda Lewis opened the festival; a small figure dressed in black top and white trousers, accompanied by her band, Robert Ahwai (guitar), Max Middleton (piano), Steve Gregory (sax), Clive Chapman (bass), Gerry Conway (drums) and Daryl Lee Que (congas). It is no easy task to be first and though her high, sweet voice charmed the front half of the audience, there were cries of "Turn it up" from the back. Her attempt at a singalong during her closing song was a failure. A crate of pigeons was let loose over the heads of the crowd as she left the stage.

Left: Linda Lewis; Nick Mason; Dave Gilmour.
Right: Roy Harper.

There was a lengthy delay before Roy Harper came on stage. Dramas erupted backstage. Harper threw a tantrum when he discovered that his chauffeur driven Rolls Royce had been driven away with his stage clothes in the boot; he wrecked one caravan and was only just restrained as he set about wrecking a second. He had been invited to join the bill at the special request of Pink Floyd. He eventually wandered on stage with a small orchestra behind him. He made a slow start, and, like Linda Lewis, couldn't be heard from the back of the arena. Soon, with the help of Trigger, his band, and a few more decibels, he came to life and gave a first rate performance. Songs like 'Highway Blues' and 'Please Leave The World As You Find It' are great festival fare. But he didn't look happy and announced that he was quitting England for America (an idle threat).

Monty Python's Flying Pop Circus contributed to a crazy day with an added touch of lunacy. Graham Chapman, dressed as the silly colonel, was given a hard time by the punters and eventually shouted off the stage.

I ventured back stage for the first time: it was full of beautiful people, who didn't seem a bit interested in the music. At Pink Floyd's insistence, there was a backstage bar. The press, never encouraged by Freddie Bannister to come to his concerts, were having difficulty getting into the enclosure in front of the stage supposedly reserved for them. It was full of an assortment of people, including children, dogs, and even cats. Several councillors had come to view the festival and even the most sceptical amongst them, while admitting it wasn't their scene, were impressed with the organisation…(they obviously hadn't spoken to the press). They thought every eventuality had been catered for and all departments were reinforced in case something went wrong!

Above: Col. Graham Chapman waves his baton at the rampant silliness.
Left: Steve Miller.
Right: Captain Beefheart.

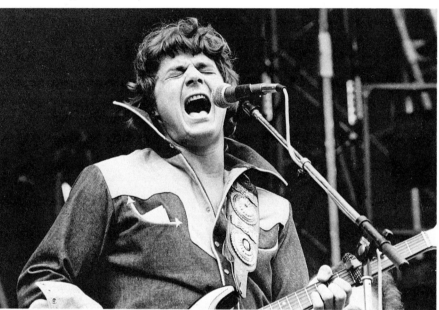

Captain Beefheart had taken leave of absence from Frank Zappa's band The Mothers, whom he had joined three months ago, specially to come to Knebworth. He came on stage in a red shirt and trilby hat with his newly formed Magic Band and he tried hard to arouse some enthusiasm from the sleepy passive crowd. He jarred the eardrums, and senses, and growled at the audience. His opening number was marred by a scuffle in front of the stage, and security men piled in to sort it out. There were some bright moments when he played the harp, and he did actually manage to get the fans to their feet for the first time in the day.

The sky was cloudy, the atmosphere humid, a police helicopter kept hovering overhead like an angry bee. The smell of large, hand-rolled cigarettes hung heavy in the air. Someone had lost his glasses in the latrine pit. Many people seemed to be asleep.

It was to be Steve Miller's only live appearance of the year and his first in Britain for two years. Having disbanded his group last year, he brought most of them together again for the Knebworth Festival. A pleasant, slick blues guitarist with a good voice, Miller tore into a lively set of boogie material, great for outdoors. Enthusiasm revived,

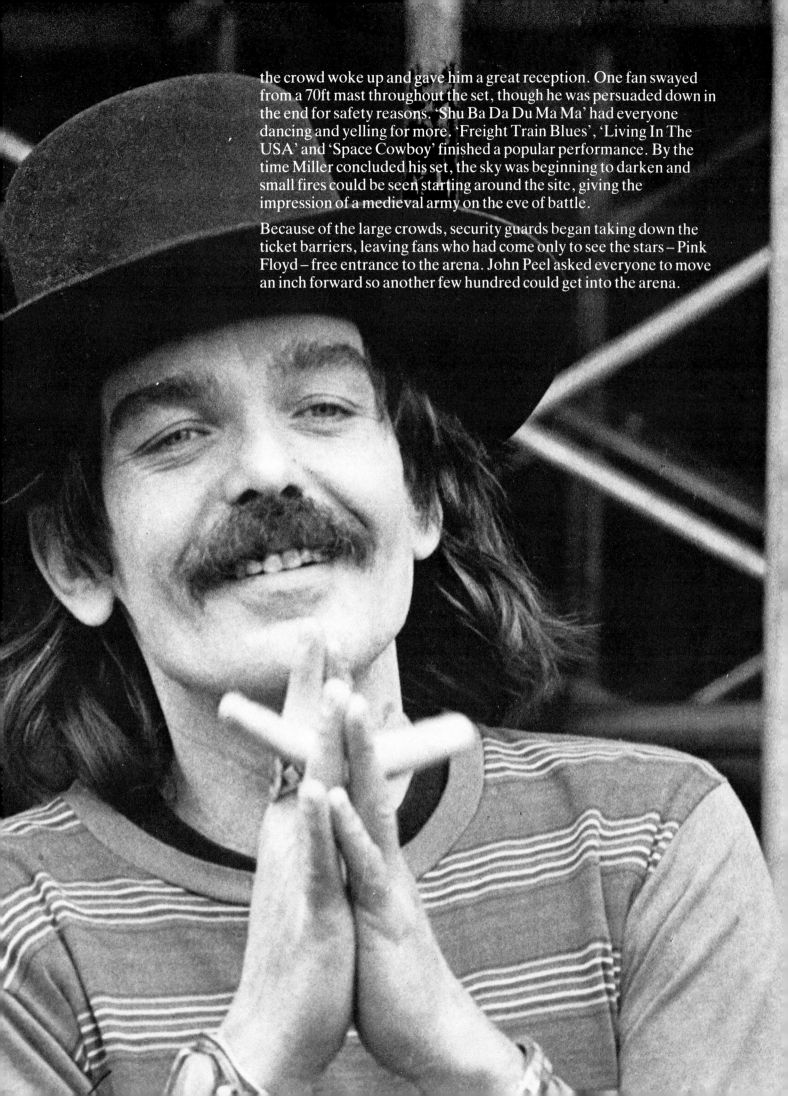

the crowd woke up and gave him a great reception. One fan swayed from a 70ft mast throughout the set, though he was persuaded down in the end for safety reasons. 'Shu Ba Da Du Ma Ma' had everyone dancing and yelling for more. 'Freight Train Blues', 'Living In The USA' and 'Space Cowboy' finished a popular performance. By the time Miller concluded his set, the sky was beginning to darken and small fires could be seen starting around the site, giving the impression of a medieval army on the eve of battle.

Because of the large crowds, security guards began taking down the ticket barriers, leaving fans who had come only to see the stars – Pink Floyd – free entrance to the arena. John Peel asked everyone to move an inch forward so another few hundred could get into the arena.

After a long and boring delay of two hours, as the sun set over the park, Pink Floyd, the number one exponents of psychedelic rock, came on stage. There could not have been a more spectacular start. The giant stage 15ft above the crowd was bathed in beams of light and at times obscured from view behind blasts of green smoke, and shimmmering volleys of fireworks exploded in time with each musical climax. Then came the moment everyone was waiting for: a rocket like projectile, held on a 60ft mast at the rear of the arena, was finally released and careered down a long wire over the heads of the crowd to the stage to be met by an orgiastic burst of sound from the group and a wild roar from their audience.

They didn't let anyone down. The show was highly professional, very entertaining and just what the fans wanted. The sound was good, their own PA being augmented by three other two and a half kilowatt PA stations on towers amidst the audience. The second set was sensational, composed entirely of 'Dark Side Of The Moon'. A large back projection was used, a circular screen on which images and films relevant to the music were projected with great precision. When 'Money' was performed, we saw great piles of coins tumbling down and tapes of jangling cash registers. It all added to the amazing show. When they returned for an encore and performed 'Echoes' everyone was on their feet.

David issued an invitation to the Pink Floyd band and crew to come up to the House afterwards. It was a last minute suggestion but they accepted. I wasn't prepared for them and rushed back to the house. The study seemed fairly respectable and I didn't expect many of them to turn up. I hurriedly searched around for ashtrays, glasses and some drink, but after twelve hours of music and sixteen hours of sitting on the grass in the park I wasn't feeling particularly bright. I had no idea who the Pink Floyd musicians were or what they looked like, but I'd loved their concert and was excited about entertaining them.

David was exhausted, having been up all night before sorting out the camping and last minute arrangements, so he went to bed and left me to look after them. They arrived and all squeezed into our small study. I began to think I should have opened up the big picture gallery. I believe members of The Who were there too, but I was far too busy to notice. It was impossible trying to sort out the musicians and their guests from the gate crashers. I would ask someone who they were and they would say "a ligger". I hadn't a clue what a ligger was but it seemed to be the password for entry into the House and a free drink. I did eventually discover that it meant a professional hanger-on, and I am much tougher with 'liggers' now.

To make matters worse, the police and drug squad turned up looking thirsty and wanted to recap on the day's events. I found myself giving them whiskies in the hall while the group and their friends were in the study, for all I knew rolling up joints or worse. How, I wondered, was I going to keep them apart? I did, but I vowed I would never be caught unprepared again.

Eventually the long traffic jams in the park began to sort themselves out and the group and their friends left, leaving a trail of empty glasses and full ash-trays behind them. No-one said "Thank you" but then they didn't know who I was either!

On Sunday the park resembled a council rubbish dump once more. Every square foot of grass had its fair share of empty bottles, cans, plastic sheets and cigarette ends. Fans searched through the debris for anything of value, wallets, money, cigarette cases. One litter picker found £100 in notes tied up in an elastic band.

Ten years later I still think Pink Floyd put on the best show I have ever seen at Knebworth or anywhere for that matter, but the reviews were disappointing. We still occasionally meet people who were stuck in that record breaking traffic jam all Saturday morning…they still haven't forgotten the experience either.

1976

ROLLING STONES

TODD RUNDGREN'S UTOPIA ● ROLLING STONES ● 10CC ● HOT TUNA ● LYNYRD SKYNYRD ● DON HARRISON BAND

FREDERICK BANNISTER IN ASSOCIATION WITH
FIVE-ONE PRODUCTIONS PRESENTS
KNEBWORTH FAIR
KNEBWORTH PARK STEVENAGE HERTFORDSHIRE 1976

Stones fans sprint towards the stage
seconds after the gates are opened.

The first most people heard of The Rolling Stones coming to
Knebworth this summer was when the Stones arranged for two people
dressed as Harlequins to run on to the Centre Court at Wimbledon,
between sets on the final day, with a long banner saying 'Stones At
Knebworth'. Unfortunately, David's father Lord Cobbold, who was
Lord Chamberlain to the Queen at that time, was in the Royal Box.
He got some very frosty looks. He arrived back at Knebworth in a
high state of fury and we had trouble persuading him and others that
we had nothing to do with it at all!

We discovered later that other gimmicks had taken place on the same day. A cricket match in Sussex which was televised live was interrupted by two topless girls also carrying a banner saying 'Stones At Knebworth'. A similar banner was draped over the big arched gates at Hyde Park Corner, but this was swiftly removed. There was an old banger race televised from up north and the driver who was expected to win had 'Stones At Knebworth' stickers all over his car.

We had great problems setting a date for the concert. The dates Freddie Bannister wanted clashed either with a major event we already had planned in the park or the Stevenage Carnival on June 26. Finally it was fixed for August 21. The licence was for 100,000 people, but there were fears more would turn up. The last time the Stones played an open air show in Britain was in London's Hyde Park in 1969, when more than 250,000 were reputed to have turned up. One can limit the amount of tickets sold, but from past experience we knew many fans would turn up on the day without tickets, and we would have to let them into the park. They couldn't be sent away into Stevenage or the surrounding villages where they might cause trouble.

The line-up was The Rolling Stones, 10cc, Hot Tuna, Lynyrd Skynyrd, Todd Rundgren's Utopia, and The Don Harrison Band. Tickets were £4.25 in advance and £4.50 on the day. The programme had crept up to six bands again and although it was scheduled to start at 11 a.m. we were worried it would run over.

The Stones came down to Knebworth a few times during the build up period to get the feel of the place. No band had done this before and it was the first time we had actually met any musicians...it caused quite a stir in the house. They held a sound check on the Thursday night before the concert, a hot summer evening. No one knew about the sound check, so there was just the band on the vast stage with a dozen or so people sitting on the grass in the evening sunshine. It was magic. Not so, unfortunately, for the battleship-built Girl Guide commandant who was in charge of about 50 Guides camping at the other end of the park.

She stormed up to the house, burst in on a meeting that David was having with the promoter and police and demanded retribution. "We booked the park until the end of the week," she shrieked. "How can we hold our camp sing-song tonight with this dreadful racket going on!" David pointed out that it was The Rolling Stones and that perhaps the girls might prefer to listen. "Nonsense, I want it stopped," she stormed. When David said she would have to speak to Mick Jagger, she marched down to the stage, elbowed her way past all the security guards and grabbed Jagger by the arm. "Young man," she shouted, "this noise must stop. My girls can't hear themselves sing."

Mick's reply was "F...off lady," but he stopped – much to our disappointment and, I am sure, that of the Guides too.

Later that evening they came up to the House. Keith Richard had cut his finger and was understandably in a panic. He sat on the kitchen table while I found a plaster. We all sat around talking and drinking and listening to their music until about 3 a.m. when Mick asked if

'There's a boring wrinklie staying called Michael Jagger...'

there was any possibility of some food. He was worried that the cook might have gone to bed and couldn't believe we didn't have one. So we all made fried eggs and bacon in the kitchen and they eventually left at 7.30 a.m. to go to a recording studio.

Friday night was a write-off as far as sleep was concerned. The crowds were bigger than we had ever had and the campsite soon filled up. We had to approach a farmer in the middle of the night to rent extra fields from him for camping – an expensive business. There was no way everyone was going to fit into the campsite and the fans soon overflowed into Stevenage.

At 3 a.m. David and I thought we would try to grab half an hour's sleep. No sooner had we got into bed and turned out the light than our peace was shattered by ear splitting rock music. Someone was playing a record on the concert stage in the park at full volume.

The telephone by our bed rang instantly. First it was a neighbour from a mile away in a very irate state, then the police. David leapt out of bed, jumped into the car and dashed to the stage. There he found The Rolling Stone's manager in a raging temper, complaining that nothing was ready and he could not find the promoter, Freddie Bannister, anywhere. The music would continue until Freddie Bannister was found.

David managed to persuade him that he knew where Freddie was and would fetch him if he stopped the music – so the people of North Hertfordshire were permitted to go back to sleep and Freddie was extracted from a quick nap in the back of his car.

At the last minute, The Stones decided they wanted all the trees in the park floodlit, an almost impossible task in the middle of the night. There had been a heatwave and drought all summer, and the Fire Brigade warned us we couldn't rely on them for help. So we stored 16,000 gallons of water in lorries, just in case there was an emergency. We put up a sign saying 'No Camp Fires' and provided a few large organised fires instead. We were terrified of the woods catching fire but the campers were surprisingly good and obeyed the signs.

33

The Stones' elaborate stage and canopy.

Freddie had turnstiles put in at the entrance of the arena this year. Ticket control was always difficult because gate men are not always trustworthy. He thought he would be able to check the numbers against the tickets taken. At the last moment he suddenly realised that everyone else would be able to check exactly how many had gone through as well. Perhaps it wasn't such a good idea after all…in any event they were all out of action on the day.

By morning a contraflow system was in use on the motorway to prevent a recurrence of last year's jams. The anticipated atmosphere was somehow smothered by the volume of people coming into the arena, a vast denim pilgrimage. Hoopla stalls, coconut shies and side shows were largely ignored. The gaily dressed clowns were slightly more successful as they could wander through the crowds playing the fool.

Even special events such as a high dive into a small pool, an escapologist and an Irishman named Michael Blondini who insisted on blowing himself up in a coffin packed with twenty five sticks of dynamite, attracted only a sprinkling of spectators. The 'Gully Cleanser' was returning to the park empty to suck out another load of effluent from the loos when it was noticed by one of the organisers who was looking for something with which to fill the high diver's pool. "Any suggestions?" he asked the driver. Water was in short supply so they went to the nearby lake and the 'Gully Cleanser' sucked up and deposited enough water to fill the diver's pool. Not very hygienic, but he didn't seem to notice.

The same 'Gully Cleanser' man asked one of the organisers who Mick Jagger was. "You know Mick Jagger of The Rolling Stones," he replied. "I wouldn't walk across the street to piss on him if he was on fire," came back the retort!

The American Don Harrison began the concert. It was his debut in Britain. He tried hard but couldn't capture the attention of the punters. His band is average USA hard rock grist and was understated and unmemorable. Teething problems caused a two hour delay before the Hot Tuna trio from San Francisco, but they did a fine warming up act and some thought they provided the best music of the day. Their music was a trifle old fashioned and a bit tedious as the set progressed.

KNEBWORTH FAIR
Saturday August 21st.

GUEST PASS

Below: Paul and Linda McCartney, like thousands of others, waiting for the Stones; Gary Rossington, Ronnie Van Zant and Steve Gaines of Lynyrd Skynyrd; Todd Rundgren.

Back stage there gathered the elite of the show biz world, Paul McCartney and his wife Linda, actor Jack Nicholson, pop singer and recording boss Jonathan King, disc jockey Johnny Walker, Dee Harrington, Rod Stewart's former girlfriend, and more. In the park the Knebworth Cricket Club was hanging around waiting for Mick Jagger who had put in a request to play during the afternoon. Needless to say, he didn't turn up.

At 3.15 p.m. one of America's great pop eccentrics, Todd Rundgren and his band Utopia, came on stage. He broke a string in the middle of a song, and, still singing, deftly switched guitars to finish the song. Rundgren won the audience over with his melodic brand of hard rock. They closed and encored with The Move's venerable 'Do Ya'.

Lynyrd Skynyrd, also from the USA, got the best reception apart from the Stones. They played numbers like J.J. Cale's 'Call Me The Breeze', 'T For Texas', 'Sweet Home Alabama' and the soaring 'Freebird' which won them a standing ovation. They declined to do an encore.

There was an extremely exasperating two hour delay while 10cc sorted out their technical problems. Fans lobbed empty beer cans and wine bottles at the stage and it was quite scary sitting in the crowd expecting to be hit on the head by a bottle any moment. I chose this moment to try and get out to go to the loo. It took a whole hour to climb over the tightly packed bodies sitting on the grass. It was impossible not to stand on some. Luckily no one seemed to mind too much.

By the time I got back 10cc had started with 'Une Nuit A Paris' but because of continuing problems it sounded like Concorde going overhead. But their show got better and one of the highlights of the day was 'I'm Not In Love'. Because the show was getting so behind schedule, the organisers were planning to pull out the plug on 10cc. David Campbell was sent to do the job. Extremely nervous about his assignment, he took his time getting back stage and by luck, or perhaps good judgment, they finished the set just as he got there!

Above: 10cc's Graham Gouldman, Lol Creme and Eric Stewart.

There was another lengthy wait for the Stones to come on. The multi-coloured corrugated fencing had by now been taken down and fans were able to wander in without paying. In order to divert the crowd's attention from bottle throwing for a while, a naked man came on stage and did a dance. He eventually fell off the stage and broke both his ankles. The slow handclaps, whistles and catcalls continued. It was 11.30 p.m., thirty minutes after the concert was due to finish, when the Stones came on stage. The audience was tired after the long boring wait and lesser mortals would have flinched at the prospect of facing the mob. But not the Stones. A massive rubber upper lip had inflated above the band, turning the orange stage into a cavernous mouth with the huge catwalk as an extended tongue. They started with 'Satisfaction' and followed with all their classic numbers.

Keith Richard was prodded along and encouraged by Mick Jagger, who pouted and pranced, tearing along the catwalk and charging down the giant tongue, writhing and wriggling. He borrowed my bike but didn't use it in the end. There were constant problems with delayed echo, feedback and faulty mixing, but by the end Jagger won the day and the crowd was ecstatic. They played everyone's favourites, 'Honky Tonk Woman', 'Jumping Jack Flash', 'Fool To Cry' and more. There were banners and flags waving, camp fires burning all over the arena and people singing.

The problems of enabling 100,000 plus people to see the stage was solved by having two screens at the back of the arena projecting the acts after dark. It made a tremendous difference to everyone. Those in front didn't get completely squashed by everyone pushing forward to get near the stage, and the people behind had a great view of the stage from all angles with close-ups of the individual musicians.

After the concert, The Rolling Stones came back to the House again with friends for a party. This time I was expecting them and drinks and food were laid out and there were people to help. Jack Nicholson was among them and I enjoyed hearing a friend of mine asking him what he did for a living. A huge grin spread all over his face when he said he was in the entertainment business. Germaine Greer wandered around annoucing she "wanted a man". I offered David and she said

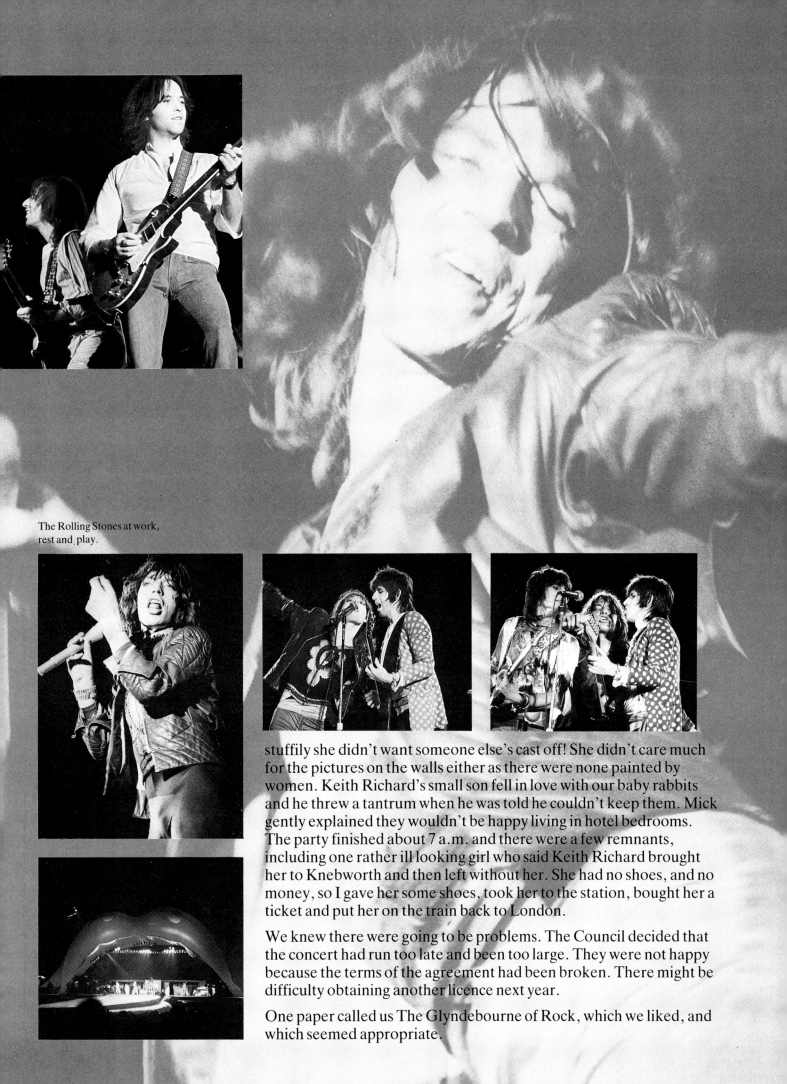

The Rolling Stones at work, rest and play.

stuffily she didn't want someone else's cast off! She didn't care much for the pictures on the walls either as there were none painted by women. Keith Richard's small son fell in love with our baby rabbits and he threw a tantrum when he was told he couldn't keep them. Mick gently explained they wouldn't be happy living in hotel bedrooms. The party finished about 7 a.m. and there were a few remnants, including one rather ill looking girl who said Keith Richard brought her to Knebworth and then left without her. She had no shoes, and no money, so I gave her some shoes, took her to the station, bought her a ticket and put her on the train back to London.

We knew there were going to be problems. The Council decided that the concert had run too late and been too large. They were not happy because the terms of the agreement had been broken. There might be difficulty obtaining another licence next year.

One paper called us The Glyndebourne of Rock, which we liked, and which seemed appropriate.

There was no concert in 1977 because, according to Freddie Bannister, no major bands were available. Maybe it was just as well to give everyone a quiet year and time to forget the problems of the last Festival.

'A Midsummer Night's Dream' was set for June 24, in spite of it being the same day as the Stevenage Carnival. There was the usual hassle with the bands. Jeff Beck was hot favourite until he dropped out at the last minute. The eventual line-up was Genesis, Jefferson Starship, Tom Petty and The Heartbreakers, Devo, Brand X and The Atlanta Rhythm Section, with disc jockey Nicky Horne as compère. Tickets were £5.50 in advance and £6.00 on the day. Sales were slow because other major attractions were taking place on the same day, including London concerts by Bob Dylan and David Bowie. No one expected the kind of crowds that had come to The Rolling Stones, and the licence was for only 50,000.

Freddie again had problems. Grace Slick, the uncrowned queen of acid rock and one of America's most popular female singers, collapsed during a concert with Jefferson Starship in Hamburg. As a result Jefferson Starship cancelled their appearance which sparked off a two hour riot in the Stadium. Disappointed fans threw rocks and bottles at the stage before wrecking and burning all Jefferson Starship's instruments and sound equipment.

Freddie had to fly out to Amsterdam to organise new equipment for them and to find out if the Knebworth concert would be affected. Craig Chaquico, the Starship guitarist, was a skateboarding fan – he even had a motorised skateboard – and we had just built a large £80,000 skate park at Knebworth. We wondered if he would be interested in trying it out.

Another hitch was Mr. Rourke, the owner of the deer in the park. Because fences had inevitably been damaged at the Festivals, his deer had escaped a few times, and his insurance brokers were causing him problems. He brought out an injunction to stop the concert altogether. There was a moment of panic, then everyone decided to ignore him and just carry on. We, as owners of the park, were always threatening at the last minute to cancel the Festival if Freddie didn't come up with our cheque. In fact it would have been disastrous to stop something of the size and organisation just before an event, and we nearly always got paid in the end.

It poured with rain all Friday, and the forecast was for heavy showers on Saturday. For the first time ever it looked as if we might have a wet festival; fans arrived with ground sheets and anoraks. Visions of the mud were not pleasant. By Saturday it had miraculously cleared up. The sun shone and everything dried.

This year's Festival was especially interesting because of the diversity of rock styles represented. There were no serious sound problems of the type which destroyed 10cc and left fans waiting for three hours for The Rolling Stones in 1976. The 1978 crowd were a new breed of veteran festival fans with an average age of thirty, shorter hair and altogether more sedate behaviour. They came with babies slung on their backs or in carrycots, and dragging toddlers by the hand. Picnic hampers appeared. Two fans set up a couple of deckchairs and a camping table, ignoring the ridicule and sniggers of fellow fans. Bare breasts were at a minimum. Even Jesus, still with his beads, left his purple and white boxer shorts on while dancing.

Left: Genesis at sound check.
Below right: Promoter Fred Bannister encounters the long arm of the law.

Folk singer Roy Harper, an old Knebworth stager, playing with Andy Roberts, gave the festival an impromptu start with an acoustic set thirty minutes earlier than scheduled, a hitherto undreamt of occurrence. His career has included spells in hospital and prison; an erratic performer with a cult following.

They were followed by Brand X, who got the concert off to a good start: a top notch jazz and rock group, originally formed by Genesis drummer Phil Collins. Fans still swarmed into the arena and pushed their way as near to the front of the huge stage as possible. Next came Atlanta Rhythm Section, representing America's deep south. Ronnie Hammond, their singer, tried to persuade the crowd on to their feet but no one seemed keen to move.

After their set I wandered back stage past the pseudo jet setters and middle aged men in satin bomber jackets, up on to the 75 yd long stage. It was reputed to be the biggest in the world and it was an awe inspiring sight to look out over 60,000 fans sitting on eighteen acres of park like a mass of sprawling multi-coloured confetti. Knebworth House was silhouetted against the skyline in the distance. I was glad I wasn't expected to perform.

Instead, Devo, a bunch of American new wave weirdos, came on next. They were one of the most bizarre bands ever to have played at Knebworth, and it was the first time most people had seen the group, who were discovered in Detroit by Iggy Pop. Dressed in white boiler suits with orange leggings, sun glasses and crash helmets, they moved in robot fashion across the stage; spooky and amusing. But they were too 'outer space' for most Genesis fans on an English summer afternoon. Their crash helmets came in handy for the barrage of beer cans and fruit that came raining down on the stage.

There was one bad moment in the crowd. One of the flying beer cans pole-axed a dancing spectator who had to be carried to the front of the arena and taken off site on a stretcher. Meanwhile half a dozen security men rushed in and dragged out (none too gently) a kicking, screaming youth and frogmarched him off.

Peace was restored by blonde haired Tom Petty, wearing a black hat and dark glasses, with his Heartbreakers from Los Angeles. It was their only appearance that summer and they replaced Jeff Beck who had dropped out of the Festival because he was unable to put a band together. Theirs was a rock 'n' roll all action show featuring songs from their newly released album "You're Gonna Get It". Petty's set brought the festival to life; the band received a standing ovation and responded by encoring with several old favourites.

After the birth of a baby at the 1976 Festival, first aiders were given a crash course in midwifery, but most of the medical problems came from the Hare Krishna free soup kitchen. Escaping quickly from a crowd of 60,000 plus clutching one's stomach is not easy, and there was the unpleasant sight of unfortunate individuals who never made it! One man had a cardiac arrest and had to be rushed to hospital.

Top: Atlanta Rhythm Section; Devo.
Right: Tom Petty.

Below: Jefferson Starship.

45

"Jefferson Starship without Slick is like Starship without Spock…functioning, but never at maximum efficiency," said one review. The Starship never reached the dizzy heights expected of them since their harmonies lost much of their magic without her. But they won the day after 'Ride The Tiger' and 'Wooden Spoon', and newer songs such as 'Skateboard', 'Count On My Fire' and 'Runaway'.

I had organised the House so that any artistes in search of a quiet moment or food while waiting to go on stage were welcome. I was mostly out in the arena, but there was always someone in the House to show them around if they were interested, and to make sure they signed their names in our ever growing 'famous visitors book'.

GENESIS

1978

Roy Harper returned on stage to try and prevent fans from getting restless while the sets were changed for Genesis. Darkness was descending, it was a cold windy evening and fans wrapped themselves in black polythene rubbish sacks, shivering as damp crept through their shoes. It was not what one expected of a midsummer's evening. A James Taylor album was played from the stage, then Bob Harris from BBC2's Old Grey Whistle Test climbed on to the vast 200ft stage to announce Genesis.

Genesis, led by Phil Collins (right) on and off stage.

The night erupted in a bright glow and blue lights shone from under Tony Banks as his intricate keyboard playing heralded the group's opening number. Phil Collins concentrated on the vocals, Chester Thompson taking over the drums. Mike Rutherford clutched a double necked guitar which enabled him to switch between guitar and bass with Daryl Stuermer. Lights changed colour and reflected in the revolving mirrors that hung about the stage. Fireworks exploded, laser beams, all colours of the rainbow, began darting out across the instruments, stretching out over the heads of the crowd to all corners of the arena. It was a brilliant performance. They really did trip the light fantastic.

It was their only British appearance this year after a major European Tour. They had just released a new single 'Many Too Many' from their chart topping 'And Then There Were Three' album. Last year the readers of Melody Maker voted them the best concert band in the world, but only in Britain would they have topped the bill over Jefferson Starship.

An hour after the Festival closed two fans asleep in a polythene bag were run over by a Land Rover towing a broken down van. They were rushed to hospital but luckily were only badly bruised. It's amazing this doesn't happen more often. Another Knebworth Concert had passed without any major mishaps. Knebworth Mark 2 was on the cards for September, but so far the line-up was a secret.

Left: Daryl Stuermer and Mike
Rutherford of Genesis

1978

FRANK ZAPPA

The second 1978 Festival was known as 'Oh God Not Another Boring Old Knebworth'. Frank Zappa headed a bill that also featured The Tubes, Peter Gabriel, The Boomtown Rats, Rockpile (featuring Dave Edmunds and Nick Lowe), and Wilko Johnson's Solid Senders. The date was September 9. Tickets were £5.50 in advance and £6.00 on the day. It was the smallest festival we had ever held with under 40,000 fans expected.

Top to bottom: Nick Lowe; Dave Edmunds; Bob Geldof.
Far right: Boomtown Rats.

50

The same stage used for Genesis sufficed. Although the bill was strong, all the performers were probably better suited to medium sized halls than wide open spaces. There were no queues, no pushing and no aggro. It was so low key that even the police played cricket in their shirt sleeves to pass the time.

Wilko Johnson's Solid Senders opened the day. The ex-guitarist from Doctor Feelgood was now fronting his own band, and enjoyed a warm reception for tracks like the semi-reggae 'Doctor Dupree' and 'Burnin' Down'.

Rockpile included Nick Lowe, Dave Edmunds, Billy Bremner and Terry Williams. Edmunds, peering out from the stage at the flags, balloons and sleepy eyed picnickers, sighed "It's too early for Rock 'n' Roll". But they put out some energetic rock and were justly rewarded for their efforts.

Frank Zappa came to the house before going down to the stage. He arrived with a six foot, bald headed, coloured bodyguard, weighing at least seventeen stone, who will always be remembered at Knebworth House as the man who ate all David's favourite Swiss liqueur chocolates, a present from Zurich. They were on a table in the drawing room and he devoured them all by the handful. Zappa went out of his way to be disagreeable; he looked at our Long Picture Gallery Drawing Room, festooned with gilt framed ancestors, and remarked "Hmmm – this could be quite a nice room if you got rid of all those pictures". He asked for some coffee. I was in a rush to get back to the arena, so I made him some Nescafe. He took one sip…"Instant coffee, how disgusting. I knew I should have brought my own," he said, leaving the rest. I felt like saying he was lucky to get anything at all, when I had 40,000 people in the park to worry about. But I left him and went back to the arena.

Chart topping punk band The Boomtown Rats seemed more interested in insulting the audience than in playing music. They played just about every track from their two Ensign albums and the crowd were on their feet clapping along. Front man Bob Geldof, rapidly developing into one of rock's notable characters, endeared himself with a mixture of sarcasm and abuse.

FRANK ZAPPA

1978

The sun shone down on yet another fine Knebworth concert, and being September it was mushroom time. I had never encountered the small long stalked 'magic mushrooms' before, so I opted for a 'flap jack' instead. I was surprised and rather bewildered to find the clouds turning into animals and chasing each other across the blue sky all afternoon; they even did it when I shut my eyes! The girl next to me took two flap jacks and promptly went to sleep. She didn't wake until the end of the concert; perhaps I should have tried the mushrooms instead!

Shaven headed Peter Gabriel, the former Genesis vocalist, first appeared climbing a ladder on to the stage wearing a white suit and orange jacket with a large toy bear strapped to his back. He began by singing a Teddy Bear song, then moved on to songs from his two Charisma albums. He was capable of rocking with the best of them with songs like 'Perspective' and 'Modern Love'. Singing 'Waiting For The Big One' he waded into the crowd for about 40 yards at one moment. The Genesis tour de force 'The Lamb Lies Down On Broadway' – the encore – left the crowd still shouting for more at the end. Those standing up in front of the stage dancing to the band were in danger of being hit by flying cans but otherwise the concert was 'laid back and far out'…lots of colour, excitement, and music.

Frank Zappa ambled on stage in his usual scruffy and cynical way to toss off a casually perfect performance. He played a surprisingly straight set for such an unorthodox entertainer, putting most of his energy into the music instead of his usual brand of zany humour.

Left: Peter Gabriel.
Right: Frank Zappa.

The Tubes, led by Fee Waybill.

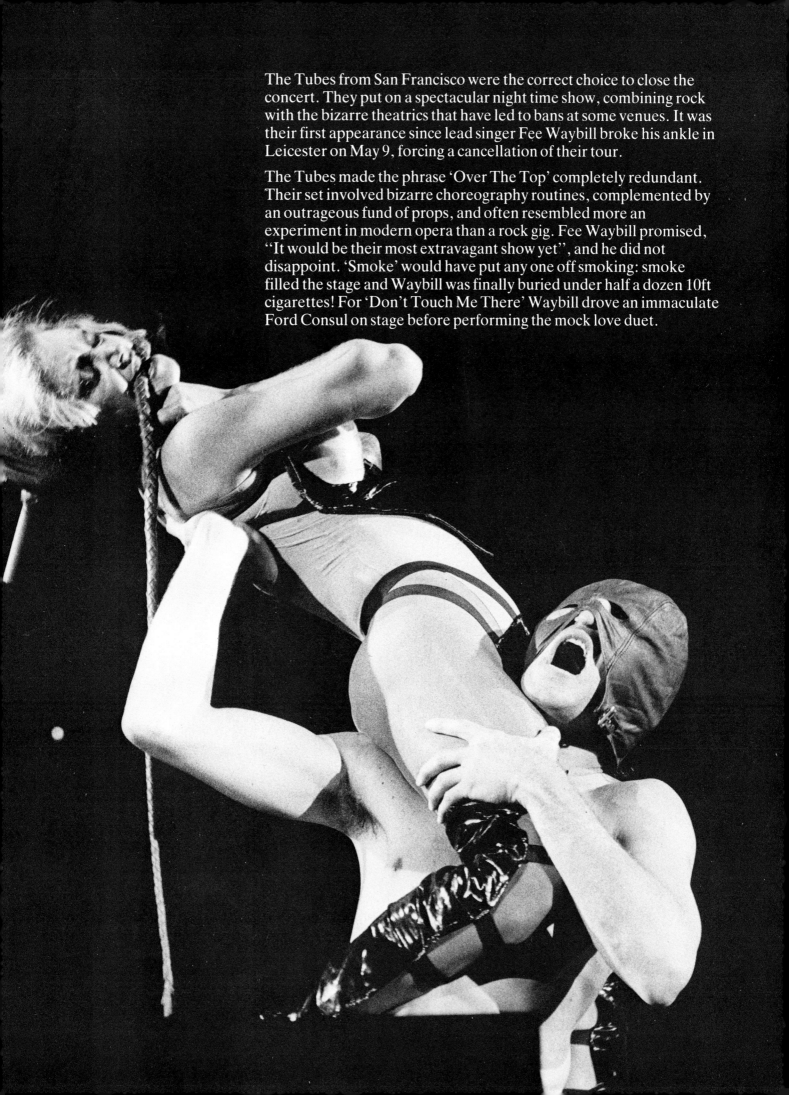

The Tubes from San Francisco were the correct choice to close the concert. They put on a spectacular night time show, combining rock with the bizarre theatrics that have led to bans at some venues. It was their first appearance since lead singer Fee Waybill broke his ankle in Leicester on May 9, forcing a cancellation of their tour.

The Tubes made the phrase 'Over The Top' completely redundant. Their set involved bizarre choreography routines, complemented by an outrageous fund of props, and often resembled more an experiment in modern opera than a rock gig. Fee Waybill promised, "It would be their most extravagant show yet", and he did not disappoint. 'Smoke' would have put any one off smoking: smoke filled the stage and Waybill was finally buried under half a dozen 10ft cigarettes! For 'Don't Touch Me There' Waybill drove an immaculate Ford Consul on stage before performing the mock love duet.

About 40 people were on stage for the finale as luminous frisbees were thrown to the delighted crowd. As the message 'The Tubes, Thank You All' came up in lights and fireworks exploded overhead, Todd Rundgren joined the group in a tribute to Keith Moon, The Who drummer found dead earlier in the week. They played a stunning medley of Peter Townshend's 'Baba O' Riley' and 'The Kids Are Alright'.

Mr Pruett, the Licencing Officer for the Festival, admitted he was not really competent to judge the music (he was tone deaf to pop anyway) but as far as the noise went he remarked, "I know of nothing to equal it since the artillery barrage at the crossing of the Rhine during the last World War." From his point of view, "The fans came, they heard, they saw, and they went quietly !"

Not so the musicians. Ree Styles, girl singer of The Tubes, was still making plenty of noise in the House on Sunday morning after the concert. She was the most 'way out' visitor to date, arriving at 10 a.m. on Sunday after the concert in a Rolls-Royce, very 'high' and demanding to see round the House. David took her around topping her – and himself – up with vodka. I carried a tray with the bottle and ice bucket. First she wanted to buy all the pictures, then fell in love with the ice bucket which David gallantly presented to her. She promptly dropped it and smashed it to pieces. The combination of Ree and vodka obviously affected David. In the end he got into the Rolls with her and set off across the park. I never thought I would see him again but she turned him out at the lodge gates!

1979

LED ZEPPELIN

58

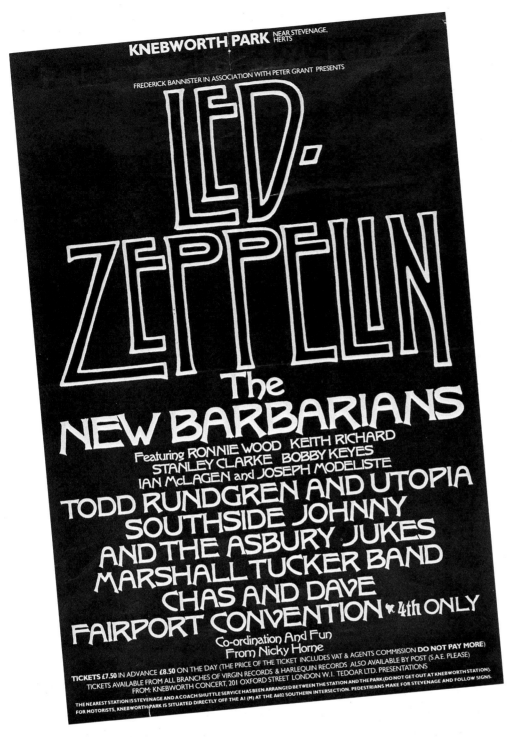

Both 1979 Festivals were within one week of each other, and heading both bills was Led Zeppelin. The first concert was the biggest we had ever held at Knebworth. The licence was for 120,000 but more arrived on the day. Tickets went very quickly and there were reports of people camping out overnight by record shops around the country in order to make sure of getting a ticket.

On August 4 the line-up was Led Zeppelin, Todd Rundgren and Utopia, Southside Johnny and The Asbury Jukes, The New Commander Cody Band, and Fairport Convention. On August 11 Zeppelin were joined by The New Barbarians, Todd Rundgren and Utopia, Southside Johnny and The Asbury Jukes, The New Commander Cody Band, and Chas and Dave.

Led Zeppelin, arguably the world's most popular hard rock band, came down before the festival to meet us and look around Knebworth House. Guitarist Jimmy Page was a fan of Sir Edward Bulwer Lytton, who lived in the House in the early 1800's. They shared an interest in the occult, and Jimmy wanted to see all our Bulwer Lytton memorabilia. He used to have a resident medium living at Knebworth and we have his crystal ball and books on magic and witchcraft. It is his ghost that roams the passages at night!

Drummer John Bonham was more interested in the gardens and singer Robert Plant nearly took a swim in our pool but decided his hairdresser wouldn't be happy about it if he did.

There was a huge build up of people outside the entrance on the eve of the concert. Twice they knocked the fence down and eventually a row of police with dogs and Land Rovers was needed on the park side of the fence to hold the tide until the arena staff arrived and they could be let in. Amazingly there were no accidents. It was impossible to visit the campsite that evening as the vast number of fans made it quite scary. At 3 a.m. we gave in and opened the turnstiles. Fans slipped through in the darkness and ran towards the front of the stage for an eighteen hour wait for Led Zeppelin.

59

Preparation for the Festival started two months previously. As well as the police, there were 400 stewards, 40 welfare experts, over 350 Red Cross and St Johns Ambulance personnel, 250 catering workers, 40 cashiers, 150 backstage crew, plus drivers and others looking after the administration. The stage, costing £50,000, was reported to be even bigger than the record breaking structure erected the year previously. The police were also charging a record fee of £50,000.

There were 570 loo seats, 750 feet of urinal and 600 feet of screening to be put up. Corrugated sheeting around the arena cost £9,000 and the security budget topped £50,000. Led Zeppelin was rumoured to have received the largest concert fee ever paid out. The expense of putting on such a festival is enormous, and it is not surprising that many promoters go bust.

Left: Chas & Dave with their drummer Micky Burt.

Chas and Dave opened the concert and for a trio they made plenty of noise. Their new single 'The Sideboard Song', and 'Rabbit', was great stuff, but unsuitable for a huge outdoor festival. Pub shows are more in their line. Fairport Convention might as well have been playing on the moon for all the reception they received. The New Commander Cody Band offered the first real punch of the day with a boisterious brassy set featuring Commander George Frayne leaping around the stage madly playing his piano. The band concentrated on old favourites such as 'Seeds And Stems' and 'Hot Rod Lincoln'.

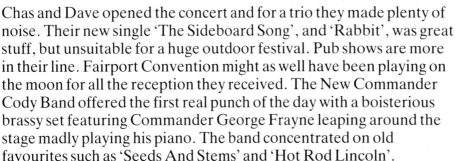

An expectant mother in the arena had to be rushed off to hospital where she produced a 4lb 7 oz baby boy. Peter Grant, Led Zeppelin's manager, arrived by helicopter. Over in the campsite someone threw an empty gas canister into a fire, and there was an explosion which burnt two cars and a van. There were clouds of black smoke, and it was fortunate more vehicles didn't go up.

Southside Johnny and The Asbury Jukes were next. For his size, Southside John Lyon had a huge voice, but like the other bands their music is best suited to a more intimate gathering. A problem with big Festivals is that there aren't enough big bands. Because the arena is so vast visual effects that can only work at night are needed: lights, dried ice and fireworks. The music has to finish by midnight, so only one group can take full advantage of the dark. To all but those in the first 100 yards of the audience the band on stage are distant matchlike figures.

Top right: Todd Rundgren.

Centre: New Barbarians Ronnie Wood and Keith Richards; Todd Rundgren's Utopia.

Bottom: Keith Richards.

The food, usually fairly boring at pop festivals, excelled itself this year. Japanese tempura, crepe suzettes, pitta sandwiches, bean sprouts, German sausages and samoosas were amongst the goodies. Food prices were controlled by Freddie Bannister, but this was not easy to enforce, and some prices crept up during the day.

The sun was setting and a cool breeze accompanied the entry of Todd Rundgren and Utopia. Todd, resplendent in a yellow leotard, put on a more appropriate show than he had in 1976: he also jammed with The Tubes the year before at Knebworth.

The debut of Keith Richard (he brought his mother, two children, Marlon and Dandelion, and his new Swedish girlfirend, model Lil Wenglas Green, with him) and Ronnie Wood's band The New Barbarians was fun even if one had the feeling Mick Jagger was missing. They were two hours late coming on, due to the same old technical problems, and the audience – bored with waiting – threw missiles and slow hand clapped. They played with plenty of bounce and drive, and there was a great moment when Keith played the opening chords to 'Honky Tonk Woman' over and over again. Any band with Bobby Keyes on sax, Sugar 'Miss You' Blue on harp and Ziggy Modeliste on drums could not fail to deliver.

FREDERICK BANNISTER IN ASSOCIATION WITH PETER GRANT
PRESENTS

LED-ZEPPELIN
AT
KNEBWORTH 1979

OFFICIAL PROGRAMME 90p

1979

LED ZEPPELIN KNEBWORTH 1979

It was the first time since 1975 (when they sold out for five nights at Earl's Court) that Led Zeppelin had played live in the UK. Huge video screens behind the group enabled everyone to see what was going on. There were lasers, dry ice, pretty lights, the lot. They played erratically but delightedly for over three hours and were proclaimed a triumph by their fans. When the band closed with 'Stairway To Heaven' not only were cigarette lighters and matches aflame, but also flags and newspapers which the audience held up like blazing torches.

Led Zeppelin returned for three encores which meant that the concert lasted until 1 a.m. Our licence was in jeopardy once more. The North Herts District Council was annoyed that their rules had been broken and some stormy meetings followed. There had also been complaints from the neighbours; one night they could stand, but two, on consecutive Saturdays, spelled trouble.

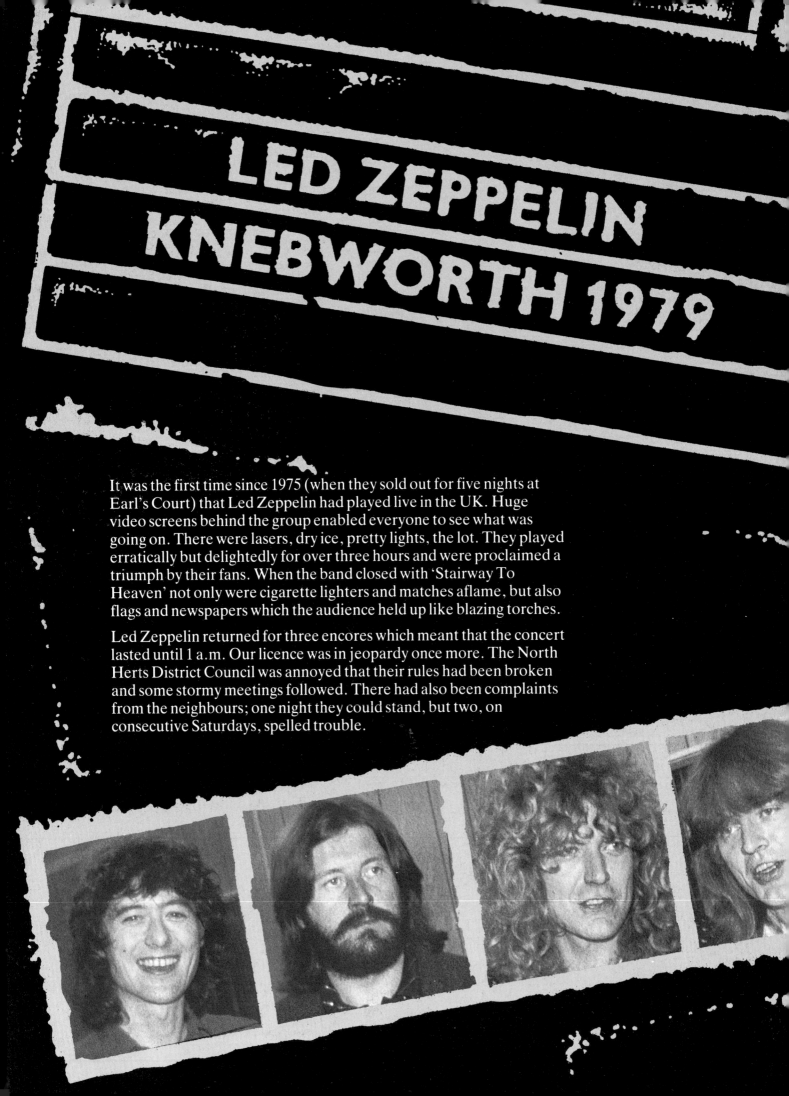

There was some concern locally that fans would stay on for the second concert. Some did, but this wasn't a serious problem as many helped clear the site for the following weekend. Litter was everywhere, and Captain Ollie, responsible for clearing up rubbish at all the Knebworth Festivals, toiled laboriously with his team of litter pickers for 12½ p a sack. They could not clear everything in time, and the following Saturday it was still fairly unpleasant sitting on broken glass and can tops. The Park was also littered with supermarket trolleys. Sainsburys lost 150 trolleys and Tesco 75% of all their stock!

Freddie was having troubles with both the Council and with Zeppelin manager Peter Grant. After August 4 the County Council and newspapers stated that the attendance had been anything up to 200,000 people. The licence was for only 100,000. Freddie said 93,000 people had paid for tickets to come in. Peter Grant, whose band was paid on a commission basis, thought Freddie was cheating him. For the second concert, he brought in his own staff to count tickets and money.

Freddie was worried, but there wasn't much he could do about it. Peter Grant's 'heavies' took over our office, turfing our staff out, to count tickets and money. David was furious and ordered them out. They eventually left, taking the money with them. Peter Grant would not believe Freddie hadn't pocketed the proceeds from the first concert. As a result Freddie's company Tedoar Ltd had to go into liquidation, leaving huge debts behind it, including unpaid bills of £50,000 for the police and £2,250 owed to Stevenage Borough Council, and it was unlikely that we would ever get another licence for a Knebworth Festival with Freddie as the promoter.

David was taken to court by North Herts Council for alleged breaches of the festival licence; overrunning was the main offence, noise and number of people another. He was fined £150.

Peter Grant came up to the house after the second concert. An enormous man with long black hair, neither of us cared much for him.

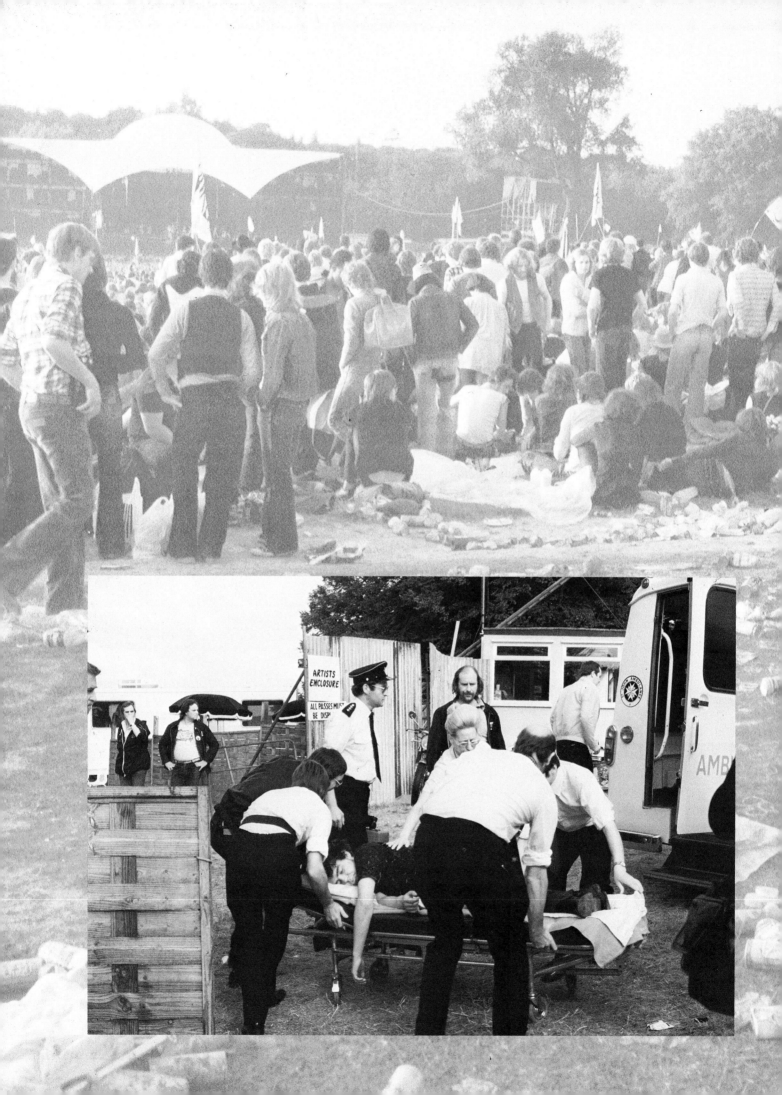

1980

BEACH BOYS

We thought our chances of getting another licence were fairly slim, but when Capital Radio and J. Lyons, a subsidiary of Allied Breweries, approached us with an offer we thought it worth a try. We obtained a licence for 100,000 but only after assurances to the Council that the consortium running the event, Capital Radio, Allied Breweries and Andy Hudson Promotions, would pay all the bills and stop the music on time. A bond of £25,000 was held by the Council which would go to a charity if the concert ran over.

The people of Knebworth and Stevenage had long since lost their fears of looting, raping and pillage during the festivals and few residents actually wanted the concerts stopped. Publicans and shopkeepers certainly didn't. We were warned by the Council that this was our last chance; any problems and we'd certainly never get another licence.

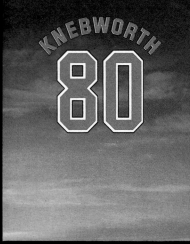

The line-up for 'Knebworth 80' was The Beach Boys, Mike Oldfield, Elkie Brooks, Lindisfarne, The Blues Band, and special guest Santana. The date was June 21. Promoter Andy Hudson ran the Festival for Capital Radio and Allied Breweries. He already had a sound reputation for efficient change-overs and timing from last year's Alexandra Palace Jazz Festival, and he promised there would be none of the bum-punishing delays which plagued previous Knebworth shows. For Capital Radio it was the biggest event they'd ever planned. Their Jazz Festival the year before attracted 45,000 over six days.

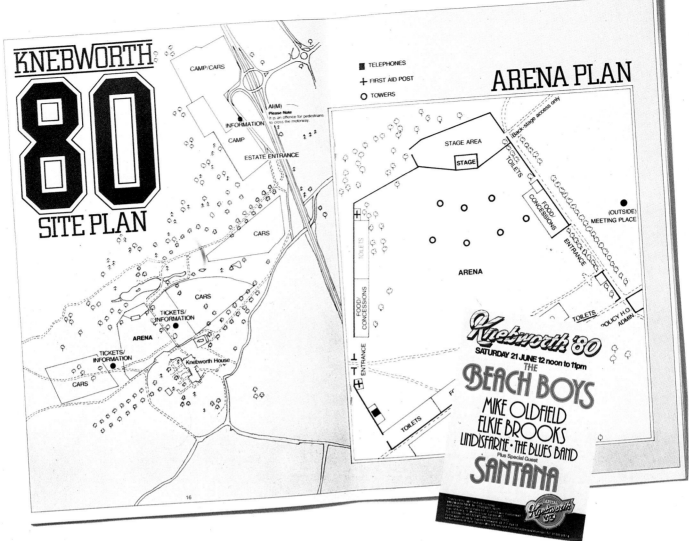

KNEBWORTH 80 SITE PLAN

CAMP/CARS

INFORMATION

A1(M)
Please Note
It is an offence for pedestrians to cross the motorway.

CAMP

ESTATE ENTRANCE

CARS

CARS

TICKETS/INFORMATION

ARENA

TICKETS/INFORMATION

Knebworth House

CARS

16

ARENA PLAN

■ TELEPHONES
+ FIRST AID POST
○ TOWERS

Back-stage access only

STAGE AREA

STAGE

TOILETS

FOOD/CONCESSIONS

(OUTSIDE) MEETING PLACE

ENTRANCE

ARENA

TOILETS

FOOD/CONCESSIONS

TOILETS

POLICY H.Q ADMIN

ENTRANCE

TOILETS

Knebworth '80
SATURDAY 21 JUNE 12 noon to 11pm
THE
BEACH BOYS
MIKE OLDFIELD
ELKIE BROOKS
LINDISFARNE · THE BLUES BAND
Plus Special Guest
SANTANA

Above: Elkie Brooks.

Left: Beach Boys; Mike Oldfield; Carlos Santana; Lindisfarne; Blues Band.

Because the concert was so early in the summer local farmers hadn't harvested their crops, and there was concern about fans trampling through fields and ruining them. The organisers were obliged to buy up one field of unripe wheat in order to enlarge the camping area.

We were so fed up with Mr Rourke bringing out injunctions to stop the concerts each year because of his deer, that we asked him to move them elsewhere. Which he did. We then bought about 20 of our own, a more manageable number to herd up during the festival period than the 300 there were before.

Everyone agreed that the middle of the road groups this year were likely to attract an over-25 age group; 67% of Capital Radio listeners are over 25 as well. It cost £500,000 to stage the festival. A week before the event only 25,000 tickets had been sold and the organisers wished they had made the tickets cheaper to buy before the day. Sales were slower than expected, but the sun was shining and they still hoped 100,000 would turn up.

'Knebworth 80' boasted improved facilities. The loos were made from wood, ten seaters which sat over huge pits. They were made by local carpenters in a building at the bottom of our drive and, as we watched with interest, we made friends with them and they would swim in our pool at the end of the day. After they had completed the loos they made a wonderful wooden boat to go on the pool with 'Christina' written on the side.

BEACH BOYS

1980

Many people rang up Capital Radio to inquire where they could stay the night before the concert. When they were told there was a large camp site they said they were actually thinking more in terms of a hotel! This said a lot about the fans this concert attracted. The campsite was ready well in advance but by Friday not more than 1000 people were there with tents.

In the end about 43,000 fans turned up for the Festival. Capital were not too worried. It was good experience for them and they were broadcasting the event anyway. One reason for the relatively low attendance was the fact that The Beach Boys, Santana and Mike Oldfield had all played at Wembley a few weeks earlier.

Compère Richard Digance opened the concert and introduced The Blues Band. Paul Jones (formerly of Manfred Mann) had stayed with us at the house a few times with a mutual friend, and he spent the night before the festival with us, so it was fun hearing his band. Paul formed it on a whim to revive some of the gritty high spirits of the '60's. They played with bags of style and panache, then came back to the house for food and drink. Folk pop group Lindisfarne followed with singer Ray Jackson leading the singing.

Below: Santana.
Bottom: Blues Band.
Right: Carlos Santana.

Carlos Santana came up to the House before the concert. I took him around the house, and he was very enthusiastic about everything. We were in the Picture Gallery when he spied my guitar (£19, from Boots the Chemist) and he sat on the sofa with Rosina, my eight year old daughter, and played for her. It was a wonderful moment and I have treasured the guitar ever since.

I sat on the stage while they played and Carlos dedicated a song to me. He tried to get me to go to the front of the stage with him, but I was much too shy. While they were playing, a couple were married in the church in the park 200 yards away from the arena. They said the background music didn't upset the service at all. The thing I noticed most about Santana was how happy they all were, laughing and enjoying the music they created.

As a gimmick and to keep the crowds happy, 5,000 ping pong balls were dropped from a B17 Flying Fortress bomber plane.

Unfortunately a breeze swept the balls away from the crowd into a nearby field so no one saw them. It must have puzzled the farmer when he found them! There was also a dog fight between two World War II planes and parachutists did a fall into the park: somehow they didn't get blown away.

Elkie Brooks came on to a storm of applause, looked like a million dollars and sang superbly, but couldn't lift the fans off the grass. After forty minutes she left the stage and never came back. It then began raining and umbrellas went up.

Mike Oldfield, in a green track suit and white plimsolls, was on next with an eleven piece band to help him recreate some of his best recorded music, pieces from 'Tubular Bells' plus many from his later albums, 'Hergest Ridge', 'Ommadawn' and 'Incantations'

With the light fading and the drizzle creeping down, Richard Digance had a tough task keeping the fans entertained while the Beach Boys prepared for their set. Earlier they came up to the House and we set out a cold buffet and drinks for them. Brian Wilson looked sadly at the laden table and asked "Have you any cake?" I fetched a newly baked chocolate cake I had made for the children, which he greeted with a huge grin. He lay on the sofa, ate the whole cake, and then went to sleep with a cushion over his head. The other members of the group had a hard time waking him up to go down to the stage.

Top left: Elkie Brooks.
Below left: Blues Band (inset Paul Jones).
Above: Mike Oldfield.
Below: The Beach Boys.

73

They arrived on stage half an hour early, hitherto unheard of at
Knebworth concerts! Their new album 'Keeping The Summer Alive'
somehow seemed very appropriate in the damp weather conditions.
Brian Wilson sat at the piano still half asleep and the group tried to
rally him by suggesting it was his birthday and shouting 'Happy
Birthday' to him. (It had been his birthday the day before). Creator of
all the great Beach Boys classics, Brian was now a sad and tragic piece
of sixties wreckage. They are a great dance band and we were all on
our feet dancing throughout. It was only through seeing them live that
one realises how many marvellous songs they have produced.

The show finished at 11.30 p.m., half an hour before deadline. From
every point of view – except financial – the 1980 Festival had been a
big success. One criticism I heard was that "The trouble was the bill
seemed to have been put together by somebody who appeared to have
been anaesthetised around seven years ago!"

Top: Beach Boys.
Bottom: Al Jardine of The Beach Boys.

1981/2

CAPITAL JAZZ

After their losses in 1980 Capital Radio sadly conceded that large outdoor festivals were not viable, and they pulled out of promoting another event in 1981. In July the possibility of London street riots caused the cancellation of the Capital Jazz Festival at Clapham Common. My son Peter worked on the site and when he heard it was being called off, he suggested to the organisers that they should bring the festival to Knebworth Park instead.

The idea was quickly picked up, and in one week the site was moved from Clapham Common to Knebworth Park. The Festival, originally intended as a four day event spread over two weekends, was now fixed for just one weekend, July 25/26. A factor which swayed Capital was that they were committed to recording sufficient material at the festival to produce 40 hours of broadcasting time to be aired over the full independent network. Until Knebworth presented itself, Capital was going to bring over from America most of the artistes involved and find alternative venues. Ticket prices of £7.50 remained the same, and anyone unable to get to Knebworth could be refunded. Unfortunately it looked like another 'loss' for Capital, especially after the disastrous occasion the year before when Alexandra Palace went up in flames hours before the Jazz Festival was scheduled to start.

Left: Ella Fitzgerald on stage and signing the Knebworth visitors' book.
Right: Chuck Berry.

This year's Festival included Ella Fitzgerald, Art Pepper and Barbara Thompson's Paraphernalia, Chuck Berry, Muddy Waters, George Melly, Zoot Money, Humphrey Lyttleton and Sarah Vaughan. Although it was Britain's biggest ever Jazz Festival, there was no need for a special licence as they didn't expect to get more than 10,000 people a day...quite a change from rock festivals!

George Wein, of Newport Jazz Festival fame, was the booker of the jazz, and Andy Hudson was stage and site manager. We had a family wedding in Knebworth House that day. Many of our guests went down to listen to the event in their morning suits and top hats.

Ella Fitzgerald came to the House for tea before her show. We are all great fans of hers and the children hung her cup (with her lipstick on the rim) on a hook in the dining room, where it hangs to this day.

The event was a great success. Whole families came with their ground sheets and sandwiches, even their dogs. There were babies, leather jacketed teenagers and pensioners basking in the sunshine. Picnic tables creaked with wine bottles and quiche, families with deckchairs and prams rubbed shoulders with middle aged couples with shooting sticks and hampers; sports jackets, comfy cords and smart wellies were the order of the day.

Top: B.B. King.
Right: Illinois Jacquet.
Left: Wynton Marsalis.

3,500 people turned up on the Saturday, and 8,000 on the Sunday. Two stages were used to keep the music continuous and ensure the festival ran on schedule. Police presence was minimal, partly because they were all in Hitchin expecting a riot! There were 1,500 Girl Guides camping in the park that weekend from all over the world; but despite some parents fears there was never any danger to them – although someone stole their pennant! Paul Channon, Minister for the Arts, came down to open the Festival. We entertained him and John Whitney, managing director of Capital Radio, in the House afterwards. Paul Jones of The Blues Band, also a jazz enthusiast, came down to stay for the weekend too.

Jazz Queen Ella Fitzgerald won the weekend for me. She appeared at sunset in a glorious long deep pink dress and after wooing us with love songs and belting out old favourites such as 'Ain't Misbehavin' and 'Let's Do It', she lifted the crowd to its feet for an ovation which lasted several minutes.

I sat on the stage throughout vintage rocker Chuck Berry's performance and Muddy Water's electric blues. Everyone was on their feet dancing and the atmosphere was very relaxed compared to a rock festival. There was no big top star to be pandered to. Everyone was a star and jazz musicians are a cheerful and happy crowd of people: they really seem to play for the enjoyment of it all.

By February 1982 Capital, in association with Chiltern Radio, decided to put on another Jazz Festival in the park in July. There were to be two weekends of jazz, costing £300,000. There were two stages, smart Portaloos with basins, and instead of the usual corrugated fencing, a double row of wooden fences around the arena.

Each day was to have a special theme with soul and blues on the first Saturday, jazz, funk and rock on Sunday, the Giants of Jazz the following Saturday, and big bands on the final day. Capital promised to present the strongest line-up of jazz artistes ever seen in the U.K. Tickets for the festival were £7.50 or £10.00 on the day.

Saturday July 17 featured B.B. King, Jimmy Cliff, The Benny Golson and Art Farmer Jazztet, Jay McShann, The Red Norvo/Tal Farlow Trio, The Bobby Lamb/Ray Premru Big Band, The Ronnie Scott Quintet, Johnny Griffin, and The G.B. Blues Company.

Sunday July 18 featured The Crusaders, Dizzy Gillespie, Spyro Gyra, Eric Gale, Dick Hyman's Classic Jazz Band, Chico Freeman, The National Youth Jazz Orchestra, Georgie Fame and Marian Montgomery, Ian Carr's Nucleus and Shakatak.

Saturday July 24 featured Ray Charles, The Gerry Mulligan Big Band, M.J.Q., Carmen MacRae, Freddie Hubbard/Ron Carter, Midnite Follies, Clark Terry, The Pizza Express All Stars and Dave Bitelli's Onward Internationals.

Sunday July 25 featured Benny Goodman, The Lionel Hampton Big Band, Dave Brubeck, Great Guitars, Barney Kessel, Herb Ellis, Charlie Byrd, Steps, Mike Brecker, Peter Erskine, Eddie Gomez, Don Grolnick, Mike Mainieri, The Wynton Marsalis Quartet, Art Blakey, Morrissey Mullen, Zoot Money and The Breakfast Band. No less than 40 Bands!

I spent most of the four days either on stage or in the arena. There were moments when I was needed in the House, such as when the MJQ arrived straight from the airport to play while another car took all their suitcases to their London Hotel by mistake. They didn't have any clothes to wear for their performance. After a general panic the suitcases arrived without keys to open them. There was no time to fetch them from London so I searched the house from top to bottom and found about 200 assorted keys, none of which would open the locks. They refused to allow the locks to be broken and also refused to go on stage without their correct clothes. Eventually one of my children managed to unlock one of the cases and they did appear on stage in time.

B.B. King is my favourite blues musician. I pushed my way to the front of the crowd to listen to songs like 'How Blue Can You Get' and 'Night Life', then rushed back stage to catch him coming off in order to get his autograph. Jazz legend Benny Goodman had a problem. He refused to have any amplification, which is all very well in a nightclub but in a large park, with wind blowing in front of thousands of fans, only the first five rows could hear him. No amount of shouting and complaint would perusade him to turn up his sound, and he threatened to leave the stage once or twice. His performance went unheard by many, a frustration which led to people asking for their money back.

Left: Art Blakey.
Above & right: Ray Charles.

Lionel Hampton, another of my favourites at over 70, insisted on dancing to and fro across the stage while singing. Sitting on a prop at the side of the stage, I overheard his manager shouting at him: "Sit down you silly old fool, you'll fall off stage." But he took no notice at all; he is a fantastic showman.

The rail strike affected the attendance figures at the Festival and jazz fans are not so motivated as rock fans. The audiences were disappointing except for Sunday when the small arena overflowed for The Crusaders. But the joy, artistry and most important of all, the sheer catholic taste and good natured vibes of the Knebworth Jazz Festival, made it a memorable event.

We were disappointed when Capital decided that its future festivals should be 'London' orientated and turned down our offer to stage another one.

Top: Lionel Hampton.
Far left: Arnett Cobb.
Left: Benny Goodman.

1982/3

GREEN BELT

In 1982 The Christian Green Belt Festival applied to use Knebworth Park. Their festival had been running for eight years and had grown too large for the farmer's field where it had previously been held. Theirs was a four day event over the August Bank Holiday weekend. We had no plans for a major Rock Festival and assuming that the religious nature of the event would inspire efficient organisation, we accepted. How wrong we were.

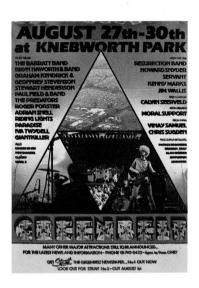

A huge arena was built around a tented village. I had never seen so many enormous marquees. A big stage was erected in the middle with smaller stages spread around. A street of stalls occupied one side. The police and local community were happy in the knowledge that this would be a well behaved and pleasant occasion.

But from our point of view the organisation was atrocious. Many performers gave their services free of charge, which meant they came and went as they felt like it. The camping and car parking, which the festival organisers were supposed to be controlling, was chaotic. My son Henry and I found ourselves at 1 a.m. on Friday trying to sort out the shambles in the park, and preventing a build-up of cars on the motorway.

Jonathan Cook, the promoter, was never anywhere to be found. He never liaised with us on the organisation and hid whenever he saw me coming. The man in charge of parking had no vehicle, so had no way of getting around the park except on his feet, which certainly weren't fast enough for the problems which occurred. The plan was that the campers would park their cars in a different area to their tents, but this was a predictably unpopular scheme and there was no one around with the authority to enforce it. Chaos resulted…blocked roads and no access into camping areas for ambulances, fire engines and other emergency services.

The actual event was very pleasant. There were clowns, street theatre, a poet's corner, zany hairdressers, and 100 hours of seminars and workshops relating to basic Christian teaching.

The music failed to impress and was far too loud. Country singer Charlene, who had a hit record that year with "I've Never Been To Me", was to top the musical bill but she had appendicitis so never made it. Cliff Richard was rumoured to be coming but never turned up, but his Christian rock anthem "Why Should The Devil Have All The Good Music" summed up the mood. Many star performers stayed to attend seminars or just enjoy the community spirit of the occasion.

Around 20,000 fans from all over the world came and went over the four days. A creche was provided for younger listeners. Unemployed people were entitled to 50% off the ticket price. It was so peaceful that four policemen turned up and two went home. BBC2 broadcast the event live on Sunday afternoon. The organisers were keen to come again the following year and with some misgivings we agreed.

1983 was the Christian Green Belt Festival's tenth anniversary and Cliff Richard would head the music bill. They expected about 45,000 people over the whole weekend. We had to apply for an extension to our licence for Saturday when Cliff was coming, as there were bound to be more than 15,000 that night. We thought we were better

Right: Cliff Richard.

prepared than the year before and hired a professional car parking firm to handle the camping and parking. We had not reckoned on the firm being totally incompetent. To make matters worse one of the promoters decided to make a little parking money on the side on the Thursday night.

The Festival was not due to start until 12 p.m. on Friday, but many people were in the park by Thursday. Music blared out at full blast around 10 p.m. and my telephone immediately started ringing with complaints from local residents who weren't expecting noise until Friday. The police rang and said they were getting complaints too, and what were we going to do about it? I tried to contact the organisers on their site telephone for half an hour without success. No one knew the whereabouts of Jonathan Cook. In desperation, dressed in my nightdress, dressing gown and Wellington boots, I went in search of him in the arena. I had a furious row with him, and very reluctantly they agreed to stop the unscheduled concert and to pay all the proceeds to our parish church.

The weekend was hot and sunny and the next crisis was over the water supply. Pop fans come and go without much need of water, but Christians need flush loos, water for washing themselves and their dishes and even nappies which hung on lines strung between tent poles to dry. Water tankers worked night and day to keep them supplied. Our own water tank, supplied by the mains, dried up. There were complaints all round, especially from the neighbouring pig farmer who gets his water supply after us.

On Saturday night the crowds poured in to hear Cliff Richard. He came up to the House first and we showed him round and he had a drink. We told everyone how important it was not to overrun the music licence into Sunday morning. But, typical of the Green Belt organisation, they ran late and instead of taking the sensible option by cutting someone else off short and putting on Cliff as programmed, they put him onstage with only 35 minutes left until midnight. As most of the fans that evening had come only to see him, there were many disappointed people.

Strict music and dancing laws apply on Sundays in Hertfordshire, and all noise must stop by 10.30 p.m. Fairly certain that in spite of this being a Christian Festival, they would not stop at 10.30, David and I went down to the main stage at about 10.25 p.m. Sure enough a religious musical was in full progress with no sign of finishing in five minutes. We searched everywere for the Stage Manager and eventually found him cuddling his girlfriend under the stage. The play started late due to an electrical fault and was only half way through; no way could he stop it and in spite of our protests he didn't. Luckily none of the licensing officers were around.

By Monday night, four continuous days of incredibly loud, and often bad, music had exhausted our patience and all our neighbours too.

At 3 a.m. on Tuesday morning David, in his nightshirt, pulled the plug on the band in order to let everyone have some sleep and peace before going to work in the morning. Our popularity rating locally was nil. Four day festivals were definitely not acceptable. It was going to be difficult building our reputation again. As we said goodbye to the Green Belt Festival, I wasn't sorry to see them go.

1985

DEEP PURPLE

In 1984, still reeling from the noise and disorganisation of the Green Belt Festival, we took a year off, but in 1985 Don Murfet, who runs 'Artist Services' – the security firm responsible for the stewarding of all the previous big Rock Festivals at Knebworth – put together a consortium to run another major rock Festival at Knebworth.

Known as 'The Knebworth Fayre' and with Deep Purple heading the bill, the line-up also included Scorpions, Meat Loaf, UFO, Blackfoot, Mountain, Mama's Boys and Alaska. The date was June 22 and tickets were £14.00. It was to be Deep Purple's only 1985 appearance in Britain since re-forming the previous year.

Left: Scorpions.

DEEP PURPLE

1985

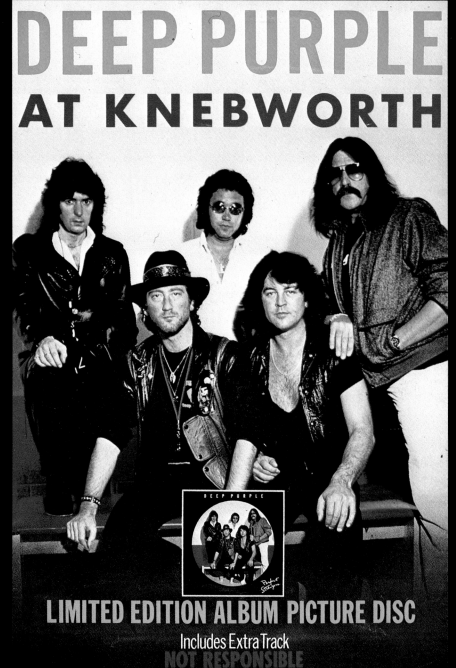

Leslie West of Mountain.

We got a licence for 120,000 people, mainly because Andy Hudson was to be site manager. He had earned himself a good reputation with the Council for his management of the Beach Boys concert and the Jazz Festivals. The licence was conditional upon all the local authorities being satisfied with arrangements and the biggest obstacle to the feasibility of the concert was a police bill estimated at £60,000. The police argued that they now had 'bands' – fixed charges for varying attendance levels in Hertfordshire – and for 75,000 to 120,000 people the number of police needed would cost £60,000. We argued that there had never been any trouble at Knebworth Festivals in the past and few arrests, and that Artist Services would provide 300 men to look after security within the park and arena. We didn't need 450 policemen as well, and we certainly couldn't afford to pay that much for them. It also seemed very unfair as no other county charged such high sums for police attendance.

Left: Blackfoot.
Right: Meatloaf.

In spite of numerous meetings, neither side budged and in desperation we took the police to Court, nine days before the Festival was due to open. The Judge, summing up, fully sympathised with our point of view, but decided that on points of law the police won. Our existing licence was therefore invalid, so there we were, eight days before the concert, with no licence. A hurriedly called Council meeting took place the next day, and our licence was returned to us on the condition that the police were paid in advance. By this time the attendance looked to be under 75,000, so the police dropped their charges to £30,000, which was an improvement but we still thought it too expensive. They also expected marquees, food and their own toilet facilities. At first they demanded a contraflow system on the motorway with signs costing £7,000 but in the end they used cones.

Another condition was that only 105,000 tickets could be sold in advance, at which point the concert would be advertised as 'sold out'. There would then be some room to accommodate those who turned up on the day. We tried hard to get a drinks licence, but were twice turned down. I felt that fans would drink less if they could buy alcohol on site. When they bring it with them by the bottle, they feel they have to drink it all so as to avoid carrying it home again. If drink is provided on site, they have to queue and then buy it by the glass, and are therefore less likely to get drunk. But the officials don't think that way.

Advertisements and posters read 'No camping, no bottles, no cameras, no tapes etc'. I felt like adding 'no fun'. It was a bad omen, I thought, and sounded negative. My son, Peter, and some of his friends were roadies for the festival, and worked on the fences and loos. There was a campsite inside the park but we hoped not too many would turn up. The first fans arrived on Monday before the concert and found the best spot to camp. By Friday they were pouring in despite the damp weather. The arena was opened at 10 a.m. (as agreed with the police in case the campsite became too full) but few bothered to go in until morning.

We erected a tent near the front the night before and I went down around 7 a.m. to find a couple of thousand damp and cold fans sitting in front of the stage. I handed round some brandy and asked some fans to keep an eye on our pitch for me. We sat down there from about 9 a.m. until midday, but as soon as the first group, Alaska, came on everyone stood up and remained standing for 12 hours. They also threw bottles continually (I saw now why glass wasn't allowed) back and forth. To start with, the bottles had remnants of beer or cider in them; later, when people found it difficult to get out of the tightly packed crowds, they contained pee, which was very unpleasant. With bottle throwing and permanent standing, we gave up the arena. For the first time in eleven years it had become thoroughly inhospitable. The fans were nearly all male and there were certainly no children around. Also, for the first time, there was a guest enclosure with a good view of the stage. I retreated there, and was invited to a few private hospitality tents for drinks.

Top left: Scorpions.
Centre: UFO.
Top right: Deep Purple's Ritchie Blackmore shelters from the rain.

Backstage was less colourful than usual on account of the rain. There were Portacabins for all the groups: one each, with two for Scorpions, and five for Deep Purple. Not only did they need one each but two members of the group had a row and one of the cabins had to be turned round at the last minute so they couldn't see each other. There had even been requests for the cabin to be wood panelled but this extravagance never happened.

The weather went from bad to worse, and the mud was a nightmare but the fans kept arriving. Despite U2 playing at Milton Keynes and the Glastonbury Festival the same weekend, the numbers eventually topped the 75,000 mark. The police expected most of the traffic to come from the south, but, in fact, more fans arrived from the heavy metal heartland in the north. There was a moment of panic when we thought 'The Convoy' might turn up, but luckily they stayed around Stonehenge.

DEEP PURPLE

1985

Meanwhile, Blackfoot, Mountain, Mama's Boys and UFO played on stage. All seemed to go down well, but it wasn't until Meat Loaf arrived that things began to liven up. There was speculation as to whether he would be fit enough to play as he had recently fallen on stage in Australia and broken his leg. I stood at the side of the stage and watched him limp on; it can't have been easy for him. The performance was out of tune, out of breath, and eventually out of favour with the crowd. The songs they played came mostly from 'Bat Out Of Hell'. It seemed to me that each time Meat Loaf shouted "fuck" – which was fairly often – a shower of mud and bottles came hurtling on to the stage, splattering everyone and making the floor so slippery that Meat Loaf fell over. I feared for his broken leg. It was the most aggressive set I have ever watched. I was amazed.

Radio One recorded the highlights from the festival to be aired during a 3 1/2 hour blockbuster the following Saturday.

Left: Deep Purple.
Above and below: Meatloaf.
Right: Scorpions.

I made my way back to the guest enclosure for the rest of the concert, and found a table with its legs sunk in the mud to stand on so as to get a better view. Scorpions, heavy metal's answer to Bucks Fizz, gave an over the top performance and looked as if they were enjoying themselves as well. Colourfully dressed, they were led by the power and passion of guitarist Rudolf Schenker and balding vocalist Klaus Meine. They played some fine rock and benefited from the first decent sound mix of the day. They literally threw themselves around the stage and were superb.

After a cold and wet two hour wait and a lot of mopping up on stage, Deep Purple – Roger Glover, Jon Lord, Ian Paice, Ritchie Blackmore and vocalist Ian Gillan – arrived. Since they disbanded ten years ago their prolonged absence has elevated a respectable reputation into a legend. Perhaps predictably, the unrealistically high expectation for this first British appearance since their re-grouping last year resulted in disappointment. They had planned to play at 120 decibels but were ordered to keep within the legal limit of 90 decibels. It did creep up a bit, allowing the full impact of such Deep Purple gems as 'Highway Star', 'Strange Kinda Woman' and 'Knocking At Your Backdoor'. After two encores Gillan announced "You're amazing, you really are" and all went into a 75,000 strong sing-a-long version of 'Smoke On The Water'. The highlight of the day was a stunning light show, lasers and spotlights, and a climax with £15,000 worth of fireworks. It was the most spectacular firework display I ever expect to see: it went on and on. Neighbours thought a war had started.

There followed an exhausting night, trying to get everyone out of the mud. Farmers came with their tractors and worked until morning, pulling cars and coaches out of the quagmire. We had angry letters from coach companies the following week, claiming recompense for the state of the inside of their vehicles, as fans had tramped through the bog before getting into them to go home.

The consortium running the Festival was Paul Loasby for Spontaneous Ltd. in association with Pace Concerts and by arrangement with Park Productions. It was all a bit of a mouthful and difficult to know who to send the outstanding bills to. We hope they will get paid in the end.

Above: Ritchie Blackmore.
Below: Deep Purple on stage.